To Glen James,
A friend and collector
of singular passion

*'Up the airy mountain,
Down the rushy glen'*

Copyright © Chris Beetles Ltd 2025
8 & 10 Ryder Street, St James's
London SW1Y 6QB
020 7839 7551
gallery@chrisbeetles.com
www.chrisbeetles.com

ISBN 978-1-914906-16-9

Cataloguing in publication data is available from the British Library

A Chris Beetles Gallery Publication

With contributions by Chris Beetles, Alexander Beetles,
Phoebe Bowsher, Edina Horvathova and Fiona Nickerson
Edited by Chris Beetles, Alexander Beetles,
Fiona Nickerson and Pascale Oakley-Birch
Design by Pascale Oakley-Birch
Photography by Alper Goldenberg and Giulio Sheaves
Reproduction by www.cast2create.com
Colour separation and printing by Geoff Neal Litho Limited

Front cover:
William Charles Thomas Dobson,
Long as there's a sun that sets [10]

Front endpaper:
Hector Caffieri, *A Quiet Afternoon, Poole Harbour* [70]

This page:
S R Badmin, *The River Dee from Creag Choinnich* [detail of 107]

Title page:
George Sheringham, *A Dragon Passing over Travellers* [89a]

Page 159:
Jessie Dunlop, *Dawn* [detail of 104]

Back endpaper:
Melissa Scott-Miller, *Beginning of Spring, Islington* [156]

Back cover:
Albert Goodwin, *Venice* [55]

Chris Beetles Summer Show 2025

CHRIS BEETLES GALLERY

JOHN RUSSELL

John Russell (1745-1806)

John Russell was one of England's leading portrait painters, who enjoyed critical acclaim and financial success comparable to his friend and contemporary, Sir Joshua Reynolds. He produced technically and aesthetically brilliant works in pastel, using a *sfumato* effect achieved by blurring with the finger and crayon.

John Russell was born on 29 March 1745 in Guildford, the second child of John Russell and Ann Parvish. His father was an artist, book and print-seller and served five times as Mayor of Guildford. John Russell was educated at the Royal Grammar School in Guildford, before winning premiums at the Society of Arts in 1759 and 1760. He was then apprenticed to the artist Francis Cotes (1726-1770), who would become one of the founding members of the Royal Academy in 1768. Cotes became a close friend and mentor to Russell, and as one of England's pioneering pastel painters, introduced the technique to him, influenced by the work of the Italian pastel artist Rosalba Carriera (1673-1757).

The close relationship between John Russell and Cotes was strained by one of the most significant moments in Russell's life – his conversion to a strict observation of Methodism from 1764. Russell embraced his religious convictions with militant evangelicalism. In 1767, whilst painting the portrait of Lord Montagu at Cowdray House in West Sussex, Russell was said to have upset not only the staff of the household but also the many Anglicans and Catholics of the local area with his fanaticism to such an extent, that he was refused accommodation at all the inns in Midhurst. His diary revealed that throughout his life he refused to work on a Sunday nor allow anyone into his studio, and was often reluctant to go out to dinner in case he heard 'loose and blasphemous conversation'.

In 1768, John Russell set up his own studio in Portland Street where, the following year, he painted an oil portrait of the notorious forger Dr William Dodd. The same year, he was introduced to Selina Hastings, Countess of Huntingdon and a fellow Methodist, who attempted unsuccessfully to persuade Russell to abandon painting and join her at her religious community and training school in Trevecca, Wales.
On 5 February 1770, he married Hannah Faden, the daughter of a Charing Cross map and print-seller whom he had converted, and they moved to Mortimer Street, Cavendish Square, and later to Newman Street. Together they would have twelve children.

By 1769, John Russell was working increasingly in pastel rather than oil and achieved growing success in this medium. He exhibited at the inaugural exhibition of the Royal Academy in 1769 and the following year showed two works there, *Portrait of George Whitefield* and *Aquarius*, the latter of which was awarded the Royal Academy's Gold Medal. He would continue to exhibit at the Royal Academy annually until his death. Also in 1770, he painted the portrait of an eleven-year-old William Wilberforce (now in the collections of the National Portrait Gallery). In 1772, Russell published a handbook to the art of pastel painting, *Elements of Painting with Crayons*. The work was revised and enlarged in 1777 and became a popular guide throughout the following century. Married life at this time seemed to have softened his religious zeal and he began to socialise more regularly. He was a good friend of his contemporary Sir Joshua Reynolds, and was a regular attendee at Royal Academy functions, the Literary Club and the Dilettanti Society. His portraits, particularly of young children with dogs, cats and other animals, became in high demand and he produced hundreds over the following years, many of which he exhibited at the Royal Academy. From 1781, he began experimenting with painting miniatures, and exhibited nine at the Royal Academy over the next five years. In 1788, Russell was elected a Royal Academician. The following year, as a result of his portraits of the King's physician, Dr Willis, and Queen Charlotte and her family, Russell was appointed painter to the King, the Prince of Wales, and the Duke of York.

John Russell was also a keen amateur astronomer. His interest in the subject had begun as a young man when he viewed the moon through a telescope belonging to his friend, the sculptor John Bacon. He produced his first drawing of the moon based on this experience in 1764 and developed several highly detailed works on the moon. Portraits he would produce of astronomers and scientific figures often featured astronomic props; in his 1788 portrait of President of the Royal Society Sir Joseph Banks, the subject is holding one of Russell's moon maps, and his 1794 portrait of Sir William Herschel features the German astronomer holding a diagram of Uranus and its satellites.

John Russell's prolific output, combined with the Royal patronage bestowed on him from 1789, ensured he enjoyed relative comfort and affluence throughout his life. He remained employed and in demand to the end of his life, and was able to charge similarly high prices as his friend Sir Joshua Reynolds. He spent much of the latter years of his life in Yorkshire, particularly at Leeds, though these years were marked by a number of incidents of ill health. In December 1800 he injured himself falling through a broken cellar door and in 1803 was rendered deaf by a bout of cholera. In early 1806, he visited Hull, dying there of typhus on 20 April. He was buried under the choir stalls of Holy Trinity, Hull.

His work is in the collections of the Royal Academy, National Portrait Gallery, Tate, the Royal Collection; the Louvre, Paris and Fogg Art Museum Harvard University, MA.

1

The Little Gardener
Pastel
14 x 11 inches

THOMAS ROWLANDSON

Thomas Rowlandson (1757-1827)

Thomas Rowlandson raised comic art to a new level by representing the panorama of contemporary life with almost unparalleled fluency – adopting lyricism or incisiveness as best fitted the subject. And, in capturing an abundance of picturesque detail, his work provided a parallel to the novels of Henry Fielding or Laurence Sterne.

For a biography of Thomas Rowlandson, please refer to *Chris Beetles Summer Show*, 2017, page 4.

2
A Monkey Merchant
Watercolour
12 x 9 inches
Provenance: Ruth Sylvia Nelkin Collection
Literature: Joseph Grego, *Rowlandson The Caricaturist*, London: Chatto and Windus, 1880, vol II, page 63 [ref]

A hand coloured etching dated 1806 is in the collections of the United States Holocaust Memorial Museum. A hand coloured etching dated 1812 of this artwork is in the Royal Collection.

3
The Artificial Flower Makers
Inscribed with title
Watercolour
8 ½ x 11 ¼ inches
Exhibited: 'Bliss Was It in That Dawn To Be Alive, 1750-1850',
Chris Beetles Gallery, London, October 2008, no 79;
'The Age of Thomas Rowlandson', Chris Beetles Gallery, London,
October-November 2012, no 70

JOHN NIXON

John Nixon (before 1759-1818)

One of the most notable amateur artists working in London in the late eighteenth century, John Nixon became best known for his caricatures of urban society.

For a biography of John Nixon, please refer to *Chris Beetles Summer Show*, 2021, page 97.

4

The Naumacia to Commemorate a Peace
Puff: See Gentlemen, there's a River for you – a new fancy you know and very useful in my case. For as there must be a Grand Gala I suppose Lake Serpentine & the whole English Navy to compliment Britannia with a Fete in Honor of the Peace – vide Critic
Inscribed with title and 'GR IV' and 'O woe is me I have seen what I have seen seeing what I see – Shakespere'
Ink with watercolour and pencil
11 ¾ x 16 ¾ inches

Exhibited: 'Bliss Was It in That Dawn To Be Alive, 1750-1850', Chris Beetles Gallery, London, October 2008, no 83;
'The Long Nineteenth Century: Treasures and Pleasures', Chris Beetles Gallery, London, March-April 2014, no 28

The Naumacia to Commemorate a Peace

Published on 23 July 1814

On the evening of 1 August 1814, grand festivities took place in London's Hyde Park, Green Park and St James's Park, to celebrate both the defeat of Napoleon and the centenary of the House of Hanover as reigning dynasty. Central to these celebrations was a naumachia – that is, a re-enactment of a naval battle – on the Serpentine in Hyde Park. Barges brought from the Royal Navy's dockyard at Woolwich were used to represent the Battle of the Nile of 1798, in which the British fleet under Horatio Nelson had defeated Napoleon's forces. In the present caricature, published it would seem over a week before the event took place, Napoleon is shown being blasted into the sky on a rocket. The actual event was recorded and disseminated through a series of engravings issued by Edward Orme in the souvenir publication, *A Historical Memento*. However, the press was less enthusiastic in its response.

5
The Naumacia to Commemorate a Peace
Engraving
11 ½ 16 ¼ inches

SAMUEL RAYNER

Samuel Rayner (1806-1879)

Samuel Rayner was an artist and draughtsman particularly known for painting atmospheric interior scenes of historic chapels, halls and churches. He is equally well-known for being the father of the remarkable Rayner family of artists, most notably his daughters Louise and Margaret.

Samuel Rayner was born 15 April 1806 in Colnbrook, Buckinghamshire, the third of five children of Samuel Snr, a farmer and dealer in corn, and Margaret (neé Ingram). At the age of six, in 1812, Rayner moved with his parents to London, where the family established an ironmongery business on Blandford Street, Marylebone. It is likely that Rayner's early interest in art was encouraged by his grandfather, Thomas Rayner, who was a professional artist. In 1821, aged fifteen, he began work as a trainee draughtsman at the studio of the topographer John Britton. That year, he had his first artwork, a drawing of Malmesbury Abbey, accepted for exhibition at the Royal Academy. John Britton soon began training the young Rayner as an architectural draughtsman, taking him on sketching trips around the country and making intricate sketches of buildings and monuments. It was whilst training under John Britton that Rayner met the artist George Cattermole, who would become a close friend and influence on his career.

On 2 October 1823, Samuel Rayner married Ann Manser, the daughter of William Manser, a successful London publisher. The couple had eloped, as Rayner was just seventeen at the time and Ann was four years his senior, and it was likely that his prospective father-in-law did not approve of his daughter marrying a younger man with, at the time, limited prospects. The couple settled at 11 Blandford Street, a few doors from his family business. In 1826, they welcomed their first child, Ann, who would be known throughout her life as Nancy. Ann Manser was also an artist and engraver in black marble and in 1827 they exhibited together two drawings of Westminster Abbey at the Royal Academy. That same year, Rayner came into a considerable amount of money, through an inheritance from his grandfather's estate, and a significant commission from William George Spencer Cavendish, the sixth duke of Devonshire at Chatsworth. This change in financial circumstances inspired Rayner to move his family to Museum Parade in Matlock Bath, where he started a business as a publisher and printer. In 1830, he published *Rayner's Sketches of Derbyshire Scenery Part 1* before, in 1833, the family returned to London, possibly due to the poor health of Rayner's mother. By this time, Rayner and his wife had had four more children, Rhoda (1828), William Harry (1830), Louise (1832) and Samuel (1833). Rayner's mother died in 1834 and later that year, the couple welcomed their fifth child, Frances. In 1836, the family returned to Derby, moving his business to 17 Friar Gate and publishing *History and Antiquities of Haddon Hall*. Back in Derbyshire, Samuel and Ann would have two more children, Margaret (1837) and Dorothy (1839). In 1842, the family once again returned to London, settling on Berners Street, near Oxford Circus. The following year, they had their ninth and final child, Richard. In 1845, Samuel Rayner was elected an associate of the Society of Painters in Water-Colours, and he would exhibit 29 drawings there between 1845 and 1850.

In 1851, Rayner's relationship with his family and reputation came under severe strain when his father-in-law, William Manser, was charged with fraud and Rayner was implicated. The case alleged that Manser had written a promissory note for the sum of £2,000 to Rayner's daughter Nancy, which Rayner had used to make a payment to a Mr Roe, and so endorsed the note to pass the rights to him. When the payment was later refused, Rayner's father-in-law claimed that the note was not genuine and his signature was a forgery. The court ruled against Manser and despite there being no proof of wrongdoing on the part of Rayner, a belief persisted that he had been colluding with his father-in-law in an attempt to default on the payment. A unanimous vote expelled him from the Society of Painters in Water-Colours and he spent the rest of his career exhibiting in provincial galleries and away from the more prestigious London galleries. The family lived at various addresses around London and, between 1859 and 1864, in Brighton. In his final years, Samuel Rayner lived in Windsor, where he died on 19 August 1879. He was survived by his wife and nine children. His son Richard and five of his daughters, Nancy, Rhoda, Frances, Louise and Margaret, all became professional artists.

For a work by Louise Rayner, please see page 24.
For a work by Margaret Rayner, please see page 25.

His work is in the collections of The British Museum, the V & A, and the Sheffield, Derby and Stoke-on-Trent Art Galleries.

6
Drawbridge on the Thames
Watercolour
with bodycolour
16 ½ x 21 ½ inches

7
The Crypt, Wells Cathedral
Watercolour
and bodycolour
31 ½ x 35 ¼ inches

WILLIAM CHARLES THOMAS DOBSON

William Charles Thomas Dobson,
RA RWS (1817-1898)

W C T Dobson became well known for religious and secular genre scenes that often centred on childhood innocence and purity. Absorbing the influence of the Nazarene school of German painters, he provided a link to Continental art of the day.

For a biography of W C T Dobson, please refer to *Chris Beetles Summer Show*, 2019, page 38.

10
**Long as there's a sun that sets
Primroses will have their glory
Long as there are Violets
They will have a place in story**
Signed with monogram and dated 1875
Signed, inscribed with title and 'Wordsworth'
on a label on reverse
Watercolour
21 ¾ x 16 ¾ inches

Title taken from the Wordsworth poem *To the Small Celandine*.

JOHN RUSKIN

John Ruskin (1819-1900)

John Ruskin was undoubtedly one of the most influential cultural figures of the Victorian period. A renowned art critic, social thinker, writer and draughtsman, he continues to be celebrated as one of the greatest contributors to the fields of art, architecture and literature of the past 200 years.

11
La Scala Monument, Verona
Inscribed 'Monument Verona'
Pencil
10 x 7 inches

John Ruskin in Verona

'If I were asked to lay my finger, in a map of the world, on the spot of the world's surface which contained at this moment the most singular concentration of art-teaching and art-treasure, I should lay it on the name of the town of Verona.'

John Ruskin, *A Joy for Ever*, Lecture 2 (1857)

John Ruskin felt a strong and particular affection for the city of Verona, which he visited whenever his travels took him to the Veneto. In 1872, Ruskin visited Verona with Albert Goodwin, staying in the city from the 15th to 21st June. Goodwin made a number of drawings of the city and surroundings, while Ruskin prepared a pamphlet for the Arundel Society on the Cavalli tombs in Santa Anastasia.

John Ruskin considered Verona to contain the most perfect examples of twelfth century Lombardic architecture, as well as some of the finest examples of thirteenth and fourteenth century Gothic architecture. As teacher and draughtsman, Ruskin returned frequently to monuments and buildings such as the Cattedrale di Santa Maria Matricolare, the Gothic churches of Sant'Anastasia, San Fermo and San Zeno, and as in the present drawing, the Arche Scaligere.

The Arche Scagliere is a group of five funerary monuments celebrating the Scaliger family, that ruled Verona from the thirteenth to early fourteenth century. The tombs are located in a courtyard outside the church of Santa Maria Antica. The present drawing is of the tomb of Cansignorio della Scala, built in 1375 and the most richly decorated of the tombs.

JOHN EDMUND BUCKLEY

John Edmund Buckley (1820-1884)

Working as a watercolourist of landscapes and architectural scenes with figures, John Edmund Buckley developed a speciality for historical and literary subjects, especially of the Tudor and Stuart periods.

John Edmund Buckley is probably one of a family of Irish artists, who migrated from Cork to London, and may be the same John Buckley who was working in Cork in 1835 as a miniaturist, portrait and landscape painter. Living with Charles Frederick Buckley, at 17 King William Street, City of London, in 1843, he began to exhibit at the Society of British Artists in the same year. He continued to do so intermittently until 1861, moving at least three times during that period: to Newman Street, in what was then the heart of the artistic quarter, north of Oxford Street (1846); nearby 7 Rathbone Place (1852); and 16 College Place, further north in Camden Town (1861). Dated works suggest that he painted until at least 1879.

12
Football on the Village Green
Signed and dated 1867
Watercolour
6 ¼ x 14 ¼ inches
Provenance: Eric Pearce Collection

13
Dartington Manor House, Devon
Signed and dated 1875
Inscribed with title on original mount board
Watercolour with bodycolour and varnish
13 ¼ x 25 ½ inches

Dartington Manor House, Devon

Located near Totnes, in Devon, Dartington Hall was built in the late fourteenth century by John Holland, 1st Duke of Exeter and half-brother of King Richard II. In 1559, Dartington was acquired by Sir Arthur Champernowne, Vice-Admiral of the West under Elizabeth I. The Hall was home to the family for 366 years until the mostly derelict building was sold in 1925. In the past century it has undergone extensive renovations and was between 1932 and 1987 used as a school.

HERCULES BRABAZON BRABAZON

Hercules Brabazon Brabazon, NEAC PS (1821-1906)

For much of his life, Hercules Brabazon Brabazon pleased himself as a gentleman traveller, producing luminous, loosely-handled watercolours of favourite paintings and places (including India, which he visited in 1870, 1875 and 1876). Admired by John Ruskin as an heir to J M W Turner, he joined the eminent critic on a sketching tour to northern France in 1880. Yet his startling modernity was probably recognised only in the 1890s, by a younger generation of artists, which included John Singer Sargent, Walter Sickert and Philip Wilson Steer. Through their enthusiasm, he was elected a member of the New English Art Club in 1891, and held the first of a series of solo shows at the Goupil Gallery in the following year.

For a biography of Hercules Brabazon Brabazon, please refer to *Chris Beetles Summer Show*, 2016, page 36.

14
Carnations
Signed with initials
Watercolour
8 ¼ x 7 ¼ inches

15
Souvenir of Velázquez, Las Meninas
Watercolour and bodycolour
9 ½ x 11 ½ inches
Exhibited: 'Artist in Paradise', National Theatre,
London, April-May 2010

Souvenir of Velázquez, Las Meninas

Brabazon first visited Madrid in 1848, encountering the work of Velázquez at the Museo del Prado. *Las Meninas* has been part of the collection since the museums conception but was officially registered with this name in the 1843 catalogue, just a few years before Brabazon would paint this souvenir.

Due to its size and value the painting is never loaned, and the only time it left the Prado is during the evacuation in the last months of the Spanish Civil War in 1939. Therefore, we can be certain that Brabazon studied this important picture amongst works by Velázquez that influenced his own work.

16
Market Bazaar, Candahar
Signed with initials
Watercolour with bodycolour
7 x 10 inches

17
San Salvador Street Scene
Watercolour with bodycolour
7 ½ x 10 ½ inches

HERCULES BRABAZON BRABAZON

18
Grand Canal, Venice
Signed with initials
Watercolour with bodycolour
10 x 10 inches

WILLIAM SIMPSON

William Simpson, RI FRGS (1823-1899)

William Simpson was a pioneering Special Artist, who is a visual journalist sent to record major news stories for illustrated publications. Making his reputation with lithographs of his watercolours of the Crimean War, and even gaining the name 'Crimea Simpson', he later developed a close association with *The Illustrated London News*.

For a biography of William Simpson, please refer to *Chris Beetles Summer Show*, 2015, pages 9-10.

A Group of Figures at the Marriage of the Emperor of China, Peking

In 1872, William Simpson visited China for *The Illustrated London News* to cover the marriage of the Emperor Tongzhi to the Empress Xiaozheyi.

On Saturday 18 July 1874, William Simpson exhibited a collection of his drawings of China, Japan, the Modoc War in the United States and Sedan War at a costume ball held by the Prince and Princess of Wales at Marlborough House. The display was in honour of the visiting Crown Prince and Princess of Germany.

19
A Group of Figures at the Marriage of the Emperor of China, Peking
Signed, inscribed with title and dated 1874
Watercolour with bodycolour on board
14 ½ x 10 ¼ inches

LOUISE RAYNER

Louise Ingram Rayner (1832-1924)

Louise Rayner was born in Matlock, Derbyshire, one of the six daughters of the architectural and historical watercolourist Samuel Rayner (see pages 10-11). She was brought up mainly in London, and began to draw seriously at the age of fifteen, during a long stay at Herne Bay, Kent. She received lessons from E J Niemann, David Roberts and Frank Stone in addition to her father, and began exhibiting oil paintings at the Royal Academy in 1852, but soon turned to watercolour. She exhibited most consistently, from about 1860, at the Society of Women Artists. Like her sisters, she often produced period interiors, but she also made a speciality of the old streets and alleys of the cathedral cities and market towns of England and Wales. These catered to a strong taste for the urban picturesque which developed in part in reaction to industrial development. Many of her most characteristic detailed views exploited the Rows of Chester, the city in which she lived between 1869 and at least 1891. At some stage she visited Northern France, where she painted a number of landscapes. She died at St Leonards-on-Sea, in Sussex.

Broad Street, Bristol

The spire of Christ Church (latterly Christ Church and St Ewen) stands in the centre of the original walled town at the junction of the four main thoroughfares: Broad Street, Wine Street, High Street and Corn Street.

The foundation stone of this medieval replacement Georgian church was laid on 30 October 1786, by Alderman Isaac Baugh, a former Lord Mayor of the City. The architects were father and son, Thomas and William Paty, from Bristol. As the whole church was surrounded by shops, the only external walls that needed remodelling were the tower and its lower west frontage and so the building was completed, only five years later, in 1791. Similar in style to Gibb's classical steeple of St Martin-in-the- Field, it stands almost 160 feet high above the walled city of Bristol.

The italianate style building to the left of the tower is the Grand Hotel, built between 1864-69 and designed by John Foster and Joseph Wood, replacing two pubs. It has been known as the Grand Hotel since 1874 and is still there today, a further attic storey was added during the 20th century. Therefore, it can be deduced that this painting was executed after 1869.

20
Broad Street, Bristol
Signed
Watercolour
17 ¼ x 12 inches

MARGARET RAYNER

Margaret Rayner (1837-1920)

Margaret Rayner born on 30 July 1837 in Derby, and was the seventh of nine children of the artist Samuel Rayner (see pages 10-11), and one of five siblings who followed in their father's footsteps to become professional artists. In 1842, the family moved to London, where they settled at 13 Berners Street. Along with her artistic siblings, she was taught by her father and worked in a similar style. Between 1866 and 1895, she exhibited 36 works at the Society of Women Artists, where she was elected a member in 1880. During her career she also exhibited at the Royal Institute of Painters in Water Colours and the Royal Society of Artists Birmingham. She lived for a period in St Leonards, Sussex, and died in 1920.

21
The Black Gate, Newcastle upon Tyne
Watercolour and bodycolour
23 ¾ x 19 ¼ inches

LIONEL PERCY SMYTHE

Lionel Percy Smythe, RA RI ROI RWS (1839- 1918)

The half-brother of W L Wyllie, Lionel Percy Smythe was born on 4 September 1839. He was educated in Paris and in London, at King's College School and Heatherley's School of Art. He was a friend of John William North, and can be associated with him and other English 'Idyllist' painters in his delicate approach to painting. However, he spent much of his life from his childhood onwards at Wimereux in Normandy, and he often painted the landscape and life of the area. Between 1879 and 1882, he and his family occupied a Napoleonic fortress on the dunes near Boulogne, a building which was eventually engulfed by the sea. They then moved to the Chateau d'Honvault, on a hill between Wimereux and Ambleteuse, which then remained their principal home. Smythe had begun to exhibit his work in 1860, at leading London and provincial venues, including the Royal Academy. He was elected a member of the Royal Institute of Painters in Water Colours (1880), the Royal Institute of Painters in

A Garden Gateway

In the 1923 biography of Lionel Percy Smythe, the present work is referred to in its completed year of 1913. Wyllie and Rosa M Whitlaw write 'the severe attack of influenza from which he had been suffering in the early Spring had considerably interfered with his work, so he was only able to send one picture to the Academy that year, – an exceedingly beautiful watercolour, called "A Garden Gateway", which had been begun many years previously.'

The house in the distance is the Smythe family home Château d'Honvault near Boulogne, where they had moved in 1882. The gateway links the woodland surrounding the house to its garden, and the artist's wife Alice, and son Philip, are at its edge with their two greyhounds. The dogs were just as much a part of the Smythe family; 'Spider', the black and white one, and 'Palm', who according to the artist's biographers was so named 'because her coat was just the colour of the silvery catkins of the willow'. Spider and Palm would often follow Lionel Percy Smythe on painting excursions, and became known amongst locals as 'les trois squelettes' – the three skeletons. A whole chapter of his biography is dedicated to the family's beloved pets, many of whom they rescued.

A review from the *Globe* in June 1913 calls *A Garden Gateway* 'one of the most charming things in the [watercolour] room' of the Royal Academy Summer Exhibition that year.

22
A Garden Gateway
Signed
Bodycolour with watercolour
18 ½ x 10 ½ inches
Literature: Rosa M Whitlaw and W L Wyllie, *Lionel P. Smythe, R.A., R.W.S., His Life and Work*, London: Selwyn & Blount, 1923, illustrated facing page 94
Exhibited: Royal Academy Summer Exhibition, London, 1913, no 929

Oils (1883), the Royal Society of Painters in Water-Colours (ARWS 1892, RWS 1894) and the Royal Academy (ARA 1898, RA 1911). He died on 10 July 1918.

His work is represented in the collections of the Royal Academy, Royal Watercolour Society, National Maritime Museum Greenwich, the V & A Museum and the Walker Art Gallery, Liverpool.

Further reading:
Rosa M Whitlaw, *Lionel P. Smythe, Old Water-Colour Society's Club*, 1923, vol 1, pages 61-77;
Rosa M Whitlaw and W L Wyllie, *Lionel Percy Smythe RA RWS: His Life and Work*, London: Selwyn & Blount, 1923

23
Dans un Grenier (In an Attic)
Signed and dated 1912
Signed and inscribed with title and 'Chateau a Honvault, par Wimereux, Pas de Calais' on a label on reverse
Watercolour
28 ½ x 18 ½ inches
Literature: *Old Water-Colour Society Club*, 1923, vol 1, page 76
Exhibited: Royal Academy Summer Exhibition, London, 1912, no 1061; Royal Society of Painters in Water-Colours, Winter 1912, no 627

L P Smythe exhibited this work in the Royal Academy in 1912, the year he was elected to full membership and in the catalogue as "RA Elect".

GEORGE GOODWIN KILBURNE

George Goodwin Kilburne, RBA RI ROI (1839-1924)

George Goodwin Kilburne worked in both oil and watercolour to produce highly detailed scenes of historical and contemporary genre. These became particularly popular through the dissemination of engraved reproductions.

For a biography of George Goodwin Kilburne, please refer to *Chris Beetles Summer Show*, 2010, page 6.

24
The Pawnbroker
Signed
Watercolour
and bodycolour
12 x 9 inches

HERBERT MENZIES MARSHALL

Herbert Menzies Marshall, VPRWS RE ROI (1841-1913)

'His special aim [is] to show how beautiful and mysterious is the common life of the streets and on the river when seen under the atmospheric effects which are only found in London.'
(Victor G Plarr, Men and Women of the Time. A Dictionary of Contemporaries, London: George Routledge, 1895, page 570)

Originally training as an architect, Herbert Menzies Marshall became one of the most atmospheric of the Edwardian painters of urban topography. While travelling widely on the Continent, he retained a special affinity for England and especially London.

For a biography of Herbert Menzies Marshall, please refer to *Chris Beetles Summer Show*, 2014, page 34.

25
The Tower of London from the Thames
Signed and dated 1884
Watercolour
14 ½ x 22 inches

The Tower of London from the Thames

Menzies Marshall shows the Tower of London from the southern bank of the Thames at Hay's Wharf. Constructed in the 1850s, and rebuilt after damage in the 'Great Fire in Tooley Street' in 1861, the warehouses on Hay's Wharf were used largely for lighters; small, flat bottomed barges which enabled goods to be transferred from a ship, right up to the wharfs and warehouses on the bank. By the time of Menzies Marshall's painting, later in the 19th century, Hay's Wharf had become a major centre for the tea trade, with tea clippers from China landing a high percentage of the tea consumed in London.

**In Smithfield Market
Looking Towards St Paul's, 1885**

Smithfield probably originated from a corruption of 'smeth field', Saxon for 'Smoothfield', and a market has been on the site since the 14th century, although the live market moved to Islington in 1852.

The covered market buildings were designed by Sir Horace Jones (who also designed Tower Bridge) and construction began in 1866. The first of Smithfield's buildings, the Central Meat Market was completed in 1868, the Poultry Market in 1878 and the Fruit and Vegetable or General Market, which showcased the innovative use of ironwork and tested the limits of civil engineering, was not completed until several years after Jones' death in 1887.

Menzies Marshall depicts the view through one of the Smithfield market arches looking south towards St Paul's Cathedral with the tower of St Bartholomew the Great in the middle distance.

26
In Smithfield Market Looking Towards St Paul's, 1885
Signed and dated 1885
Watercolour
6 ½ x 9 ¾ inches

27 (above)
Shipping on the Thames at Bankside
Signed and dated [84?]
Watercolour with bodycolour
6 ¾ x 10 inches

28 (below)
Westminster Abbey from Westminster Bridge
Signed and dated 1892
Watercolour with bodycolour
5 ¼ x 8 ¼ inches

EDITH MARTINEAU

Edith Martineau, ARWS (1842-1909)

Edith Martineau was a pioneering figure among artists of the Victorian period, in that she was one of the first women to be admitted to the Royal Academy Schools and one of the first to be elected an Associate of the Royal Society of Painters in Water-Colours. She was also ambitious in the range of her subject matter, applying her admired precision of handling to floral still life compositions, landscapes, rural genre scenes and portraits of children.

For a biography of Edith Martineau, please refer to *Chris Beetles Summer Show*, 2016, pages 20-21.

29
Water Lilies
Signed and dated 1884
Watercolour
14 ½ x 21 inches

30
Resting
Signed and dated 1886
Watercolour
with bodycolour
22 ¾ x 15 inches
Illustrated: *Lady's Pictorial*,
2 April 1887, page 348
& 4 July 1887, page 497;
The Illustrated London News,
30 April 1887, page 601;
Exhibited: Royal Institute of
Painters in Watercolours,
West Gallery, London,
1887, no 374

GEORGE JOHN PINWELL

George John Pinwell (1842-1875)

Regarded by contemporaries as one of the finest illustrators of his time, George Pinwell was known as a member of the 'Idyllist' school of artists. Along with contemporaries including John William North and Frederick Walker, he developed wood-engraving illustrations into beautifully realised watercolours that combined Pre-Raphaelite beauty with social realism and narrative expression. Had his life and career not been sadly cut short by tuberculosis at the age of just thirty-two, he would surely be celebrated today as one of the most important illustrators and watercolourists of the Victorian period.

George John Pinwell was born on 26 December 1842 at 12 Great Mays Buildings, London. He was the eldest of three sons of John Pinwell, a carpenter, and his wife Mary Ann (neé Barker). In 1854, his father died, and with the family threatened by destitution, the twelve-year-old Pinwell found work as a butterman's boy on the City Road. In 1861, his mother remarried and, with the family more financially secure and his younger brothers Henry and Alfred apprenticed as house carpenters, Pinwell left home to study art. Initially, he attended evening classes at St Martin's School of Art, and supported himself by working as an apprentice draughtsman at a firm of embroiderers. Whilst there, he met Isabella Mercy Stevens. They were married on 25 April 1865 at St Marylebone parish church. In 1862, he left St Martin's to study at Heatherley's Academy, the same year he began executing designs for the Birmingham electroplating company, Elkington's.

George Pinwell's first illustrations to appear in print were published in 1862 in *Liliput Levee*, a book of nursery rhymes for children by William Brighty Rands. The same year, he received his first commission for a wood-engraving illustration for the periodical *Once a Week*. The drawing illustrated a poem by George Walter Thornbury titled *The Saturnalia*, and appeared on 31 January 1863. This marked the start of a prolific period in which he produced over 500 illustrations for books and periodicals, engraved by the leading engraving firms of the time, including Joseph Swain, J W Whymper (where he met his friend and contemporary John William North) and the Dalziel Brothers. His work on *Dalziels' Illustrated Goldsmith* (1865) was one of his most significant projects, producing over 100 illustrations for the book over a period of six months. George Pinwell's illustrations appeared in periodicals such as *Good Words*, *The Graphic*, *London Society*, *The Quiver* and the *Cornhill Magazine*. His book commissions included *The Adventures of Gil Blas* (1866), *Wayside Posies* (1867), *The Uncommercial Traveller* (1868) and *Picture Posies* (1874) amongst many others.

In addition to George Pinwell's success and popularity as a wood-engraving illustrator, he was also an accomplished artist in watercolour and oil. His paintings were often inspired by previous works he had completed as wood-engraving illustrations, indeed, the first watercolour he exhibited, *An Incident in the Life of Oliver Goldsmith* in 1865 at the Dudley Gallery, London, was developed using imagery he had used in *Dalziels' Illustrated Goldsmith*. In 1869, he was elected an associate of the Society of Painters in Water Colours and a full member the following year, and contributed 59 works to the society's exhibitions over the course of his career. He was also elected an honorary member of the Belgian Society of Painters in Watercolours. Along with his contemporaries John William North, Frederick Walker and Arthur Boyd Houghton, George Pinwell was part of a group of artists referred to as the Idyllists, whose styles were developed from their work engraved for book illustration. This Idyllic School was defined as blending Pre-Raphaelite theories of realism with demands of narrative expression in their interpretations of rural landscapes and figurative scenes.

In 1874, Pinwell developed acute respiratory problems and attempted to alleviate his symptoms by travelling to the warm, dry climate of Tangier. He remained there for eight months, returning in the spring of 1875. His condition worsened however and he died of tuberculosis at his home on Adelaide Road, Haverstock Hill, London, on 8 September 1875, aged just thirty-two. He was survived by his wife, with whom he did not have any children, and was buried in Highgate Cemetery. At his death, he left an unfinished large-scale oil entitled *Vanity Fair*, which he had begun two years earlier. It is believed that with this painting he was going to seek admission to the Royal Academy.

His work is in the collections of the British Museum, the V & A Museum, and the Boston Museum of Fine Arts, MA.

31
Visiting the Poor
Signed with monogram and dated 67
Watercolour with bodycolour
6 ½ x 5 ¼ inches
Literature: George C Williamson, *George J Pinwell and His Works*,
London: George Bell & Sons, 1900, opposite page 35
Exhibited: 'The Pinwell Exhibition', Deschamp's Gallery, London, February 1876, no 78

GEORGE JOHN PINWELL

32
The Old Cart
Signed on reverse
Watercolour
8 ¾ x 6 ¾ inches
Illustrated: Robert Williams Buchanan, *Wayside Posies*, London: Routledge, 1867, page 58

Through many a year of troubles and of joys,
Strong friend and faithful has this old cart been!
Ah, if it just for once could find a voice!
Could chatter of the things that it has seen!

(*Wayside Posies*, 1867, page 58)

ROBERT THORNE WAITE

Robert Thorne Waite, RWS RBC ROI (1843-1935)

Robert Thorne Waite was a painter, mostly in watercolour, of bright and airy landscapes and pastoral scenes. He was particularly fond of the corn and hay fields of the South Downs.

For a biography of Robert Thorne Waite, please refer to *Chris Beetles Summer Show*, 2020, page 120.

33
Haymaking
Signed
Watercolour
13 ¼ x 20 ¼ inches
Exhibited: Royal Watercolour Society, London, November 1984, no 32

ALBERT GOODWIN

Albert Frederick Goodwin, RWS RWA (1845-1932)

In synthesising the influences of J M W Turner and the Pre-Raphaelites, Albert Goodwin may be considered one of the most Ruskinian of Victorian landscape painters. Indeed, he was taken up by John Ruskin and, in 1872, given the opportunity to travel with him on an intensive tour of Italy and Switzerland. This set the pattern for many further and extensive travels. Like Ruskin, Goodwin responded to landscape with a religious fervour and understanding; but he interpreted it with greater eclecticism than did his mentor, even experimenting with the style of James McNeill Whistler, Ruskin's adversary in the field of aesthetics.

For a biography of Albert Goodwin, please refer to *Chris Beetles Summer Show*, 2014, page 26.

34
Near Winchester
Signed with monogram and dated 64
Watercolour
6 x 4 ¾ inches
Provenance: George Price Boyce
Exhibited: 'The Great Age of British Watercolour 1750-1880', Royal Academy, London, 1993, no 409;
'Pre-Raphaelite Vision: Truth to Nature', Tate Britain, London, 2004, no 51

An original label on the reverse is inscribed 'Winchester 1864 watercolour 6 ins x 5 ins by Albert Goodwin ARWS. The property of George Boyce, who bought it from the artist'.

George Price Boyce RWS (1826-1897) was a British watercolour painter of Pre-Raphaelite style landscapes and also a patron and friend of Dante Gabriel Rossetti.

35
Amsterdam
Signed with monogram
and dated 64
Watercolour
9 ¾ x 14 inches

36
Above Whitby Harbour
Signed with monogram
and dated 65
Watercolour and
bodycolour
7 x 10 inches
Exhibited: 'The Albert
Goodwin Exhibition',
Chris Beetles Gallery,
London, May-June
1996, no 5

37 (above)
The Estuary
Signed with monogram and dated 66
Watercolour
3 ¾ x 10 inches

38 (below)
Sunset Through the Woodland
Signed with monogram and dated 65
Watercolour
13 ¾ x 19 inches
Exhibited: 'The Albert Goodwin Exhibition',
Chris Beetles Gallery, London, May-June 1996, no 1

39
Matlock
Signed and dated /71
Watercolour
10 x 14 inches
Literature: Hammond Smith, *Albert Goodwin RWS (1845-1932)*,
Leigh-on-sea: F Lewis, 1977, plate 9
Exhibited: 'The Albert Goodwin Exhibition', Chris Beetles Gallery,
London, May-June 1996, no 9

40
Bristol Close
Signed with monogram, inscribed with title and dated 86
Watercolour and bodycolour enclosed within a decorative border
5 x 6 ¼ inches

41
Maidstone
Signed, inscribed with title and dated 1878 and 1912
Watercolour with ink and bodycolour
7 ½ x 12 ¾ inches
Exhibited: 'Drawings and Pictures by Albert Goodwin, RWS', Leggatt Brothers Gallery, London, 1919, no 52, as 'Maidstone 1878'

42
Ilfracombe
Signed, inscribed with title and dated 1925
Watercolour with ink enclosed within a decorative border
11 ¼ x 15 ¼ inches

43
Whitby
Signed, inscribed with title and dated 1910
Watercolour with bodycolour
13 ½ x 20 ¼ inches
Literature: *Albert Goodwin RWS, 1845-1932*, London: Chris Beetles, 1986, Limited Edition of 1000, plate 190
Exhibited: 'Albert Goodwin RWS 1845-1932. 129 of His Best Works Borrowed From Private Collections', A Museum Tour of the Royal Watercolour Society, Sheffield Mappin Art Gallery, Ruskin Gallery, Stoke on Trent City Museum and Art Gallery, May-October 1986, no 123

'... Whitby, its exceeding picturesqueness ... as far as I have seen there is no town in England like unto it in its wealth of colour.'
[quote from the Fine Art Society exhibition catalogue of May 1886]

44
Canterbury Cathedral
Signed and
inscribed 'Canterbury'
Watercolour enclosed
within a decorative border
5 x 7 inches

45
Whitby
Signed and inscribed
with title
Watercolour
10 ¼ x 14 ¼ inches

46
The Avon Ferry, Bristol
Signed and inscribed with title
Watercolour
10 x 14 ¼ inches
Literature: *Albert Goodwin RWS, 1845-1932*, London: Chris Beetles, 1986,
Limited Edition of 1000, plate 111
Exhibited: 'An Exhibition of Pictures and Watercolours entitled
"In Praise of All The Churches" by Albert Goodwin, RWS', Fine Art Society,
London, November 1900, no 61;
'Sunset and Colour from East and West Drawings by Albert Goodwin, R.W.S',
Robert Dunthorne's The Rembrandt Head Gallery, London, 1902, no 15;
'The Jimmy James Collection', Chris Beetles Gallery, London, October 2022

'Three months spent at the Simplon village in 1873 enables me still to go there in spirit'
[quote from the Fine Art Society exhibition catalogue of May 1890]

47
A Stormy Sunday, Simplon
Signed and dated 74
Watercolour
19 x 28 inches
Exhibited: Royal Society of Painters in Water-Colours, London, Summer 1874, no 81

48
Under the Fletchorn, Simplon
Signed and inscribed with title
Watercolour with oil, ink and pencil on tinted paper
10 ½ x 14 ½ inches
Exhibited: Royal Society of Painters in Water-Colours, London, Winter 1875, no 35

49
Lucerne
Signed and inscribed with title
Watercolour
5 ¼ x 6 ¾ inches

50
Meran, Tyrol
Signed, inscribed with title and dated 1911
Watercolour with bodycolour
10 x 14 ½ inches

51

Lauterbrunnen
Signed and inscribed with title
Watercolour with ink and bodycolour
6 ¾ x 10 inches
Possibly the painting of the same title exhibited at Royal Society of Painters in Water-Colours, Summer 1920, no 105;
Exhibited: 'The Albert Goodwin Exhibition', May-June 1996, Chris Beetles Gallery, London, no 103

52

The Last Gleam on the Jungfrau
Signed and inscribed 'Jungfrau'
Watercolour and bodycolour with pencil
10 ½ x 14 ¼ inches
Exhibited: 'Water-Colour Drawings and Paintings by Albert Goodwin, RWS', Leggatt Brothers Gallery, London, 1912, no 31

53
The Saluté, Venice
Signed, inscribed 'The Salute' and dated 1903
Watercolour with bodycolour
9 ½ x 13 ¼ inches
Exhibited: 'A Collection of Water-Colour Drawings by Albert Goodwin, RWS',
Robert Dunthorne's The Rembrandt Gallery, London, 1904, no 44

54
A Venetian Butterfly in front of the Gesuati
Signed, inscribed 'The church of the Jesuits, Venice'
and dated 1913
Watercolour with ink
10 ½ x 14 ¼ inches

55
Venice
Signed and inscribed with title
Watercolour
20 ½ x 29 ¼ inches

56
The Citadel, Cairo
Signed, inscribed with title and dated 1907
Watercolour with ink enclosed within a decorative border
6 x 9 ¼ inches
Provenance: The Lyndon Goodwin Harris Collection
Exhibited: Possibly the painting exhibited at 'An Exhibition of Water-Colours of Dawn and Sunset by Albert Goodwin, RWS', Fine Art Society, London, January 1907, no 72

57
The Desert
Signed, inscribed with title and dated 1915
Watercolour with bodycolour
11 ¾ x 18 ½ inches

58
The Phantom Ship
Signed and inscribed with title
Watercolour and bodycolour with ink
6 ¾ x 9 ¾ inches
Exhibited: 'An Exhibition of Pictures and Watercolours entitled
"In Praise of All The Churches" by Albert Goodwin, RWS',
Fine Art Society, London, November 1900, no 4;
'Water-Colour Drawings and Oil Paintings by Albert Goodwin, R.W.S.',
Vicars Brothers, London, 1925, no 28

59
The Last Voyage of the Adventure
Signed, inscribed with title and dated 1920
Watercolour with bodycolour
13 ¼ x 19 ¾ inches

60

The End of the Pilgrim's Road
Signed, inscribed 'The river, for he shall give his angels
charge over thee', and dated 1902
Inscribed with title and artist's address on label on reverse
Oil on canvas
42 ½ x 56 ½ inches
Provenance: Matthew Biggar Walker Esq, of Wolverhampton;
Christie's, London, 9 March 1928, Lot 92 (7 guineas 7 Shillings to
J Ward);
Christie's, London, 5 March 1971, Lot 63
Exhibited: Royal Academy, Summer Exhibition, London, 1902, no
405;
'An Exhibition of Oil Paintings, Water Colour Drawings, etc.
by Albert Goodwin, R.W.S., R.W.A. loaned by M B Walker Esq',
Municipal Art Gallery and Museum, Wolverhampton,
December 1925, no 39;
'A collection of oil paintings, water colour drawings etc.
by Albert Goodwin, R.W.S., R.W.A.
Lent by M.B. Walker Esq', City of Birmingham Museum
and Art Gallery, 1926, no 122

The inscription is taken from Psalm 91, verse xi

*'Now I further saw that between them and the gate was a river;
but there was no bridge to go over and the river was very deep.
At the sight, therefore, of this river, the Pilgrims were much
stunned, but the men that went with them said 'you must go
through or you cannot come to the gate''*

(*Bunyan's Pilgrims Progress*) [quoted in the exhibition catalogue at
Wolverhampton Art Gallery and Museum, December 1925]

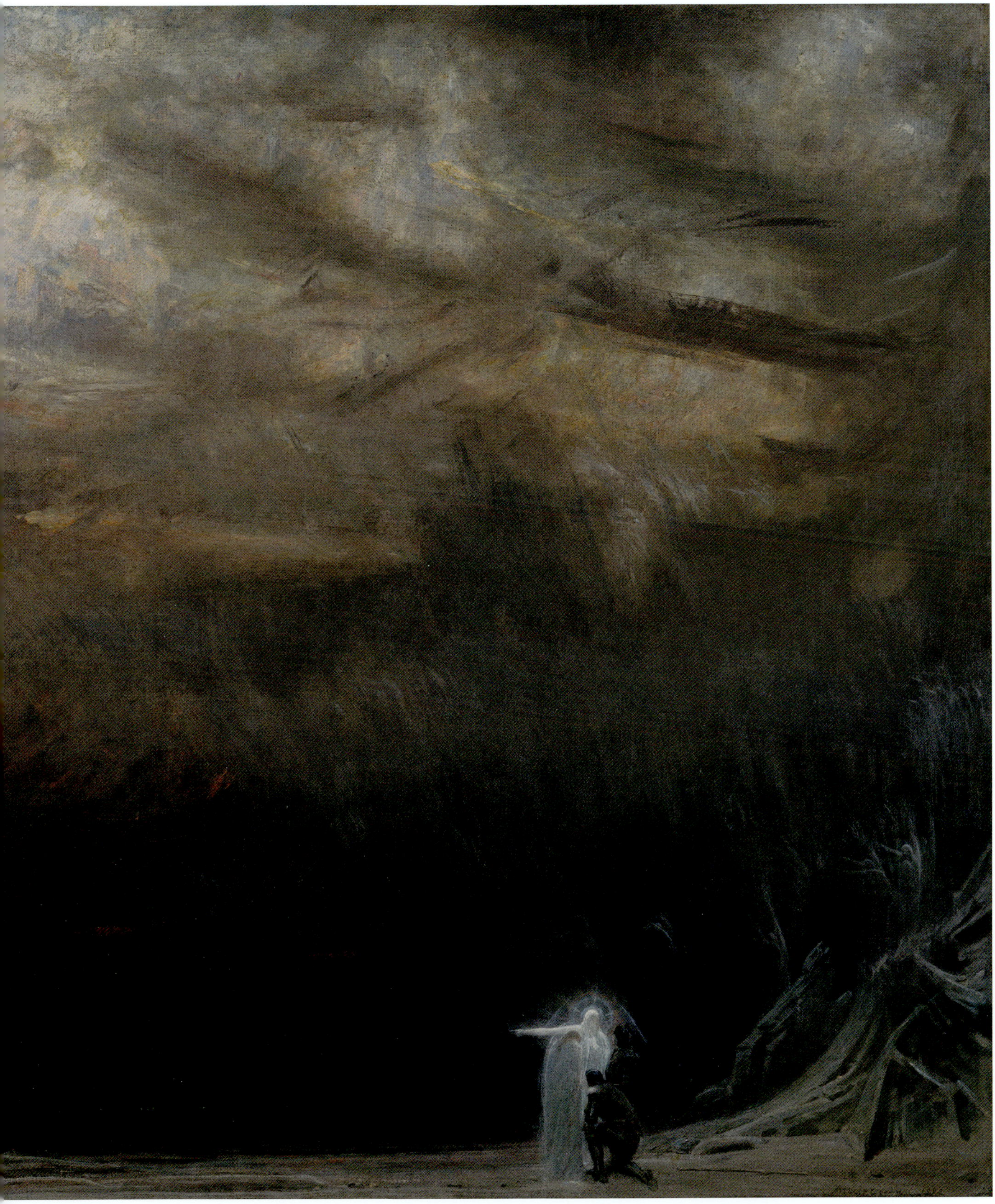

FRANCIS ARTHUR FRASER

Francis Arthur Fraser (1846-1924)

Francis Arthur Fraser was a prolific figure in the Victorian publishing world, celebrated mainly for his work as an illustrator during the golden age of wood-engraved printing. Although a regular exhibitor of oil paintings and watercolours, it was through this form of illustration that he became a widely recognised name in the late nineteenth century. He was the eldest brother of Robert Winchester Fraser, Garden William Fraser, George Gordon Fraser, Arthur Anderson Fraser, Gilbert Baird Fraser, Robert James Winchester Fraser and Francis George Gordon Fraser – all of whom established successful careers as painters. Together they formed the Fraser Family, widely remembered for their striking landscape watercolours of the wide, flat Fenlands.

Born on the island of Vido, Corfu, on 13 July 1846, Francis Arthur Fraser returned to England in his youth and was educated at Bedford Grammar School between 1861-63, before moving to London in 1864. There, he entered the successful world of illustrated journalism, benefitting from a dramatic increase in literacy, the expansion of magazine publishing, and technical advances in print reproduction.

His first published drawings appeared in *Once a Week* in 1867, and were soon followed by a constant stream of commissions for *The Sunday Magazine*, *St Paul's Magazine*, and most notably *Good Words*, for which he contributed nearly 200 illustrations between 1869 and 1871. From 1870, he was a regular and familiar presence in the satirical magazine *Fun*, producing weekly cartoons and humorous sketches that reflected Victorian society with a dry, observational wit. His style remained consistent across all formats – elegant, fluid and well-adapted to narrative – and his work became a staple of the mid-century illustrated press. Fraser reached his peak as an illustrator in 1885 when he was working for 8 different publications.

Fraser's drawings were predominantly engraved by the Dalziel Brothers, one of the most substantial London wood-engraving companies in the Victorian era who collaborated with many of the leading artists of the day. He also worked with Joseph Swain, whose strong craftsmanship brought greater depth to the final prints.

Though best known as an illustrator, Fraser maintained a steady and active career as a painter. He exhibited fifteen works at the Royal Scottish Academy (1866-1879), eleven at the Society of British Artists (1867-1883), and further paintings at the Royal Academy, Dudley Gallery and Walker Art Gallery in Liverpool. His oils reflect the traditions of Victorian narrative painting, while his landscapes in watercolour are more expressive in tone and composition.

Fraser signed his work using several variants, including his full name, the initials 'F A F', and very rarely, a distinctive monogram in the form of two mirrored Fs joined to form an A.

In 1876, he married Charlotte Susan Downie of Boweshill, Blantyre, and settled in Barnes, Surrey. Later years were spent in Shere in Surrey and Walmer, Kent. He died of cirrhosis of the liver on 7 November 1924.

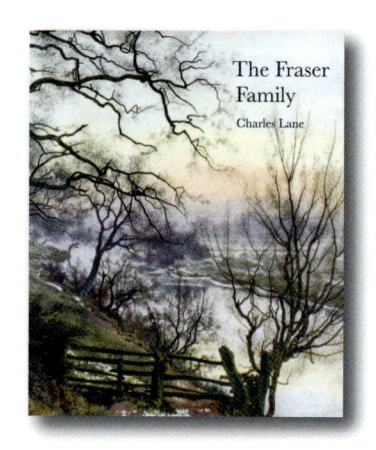

Charles Lane's
The Fraser Family

Chris Beetles Gallery has regularly shown a range of works by members of the Fraser family that has been significant in both number and quality. In 2010, it built on its experience by publishing Charles Lane's *The Fraser Family*, the first substantial publication devoted to the artists.

61
Farm at Lyford, Surrey
Signed and dated 1880
Watercolour
11 ½ x 15 ½ inches

ALFRED PARSONS

Alfred William Parsons, RA PRWS RSW RI
HRMS ROI NEAC (1847-1920)

Alfred Parsons became an expert in various branches of the art of the garden. He used watercolour to produce fresh portraits of gardens and accurate illustrations of botanical specimens. Having collaborated on books with the famous gardener, William Robinson, he went on to become a designer of gardens in Britain and the United States. His transatlantic connections were strengthened through his membership of the Anglo-American 'Broadway Group' of artists and writers that included Henry James and John Singer Sargent. Between 1892-94 he further broadened his horizons and deepened his knowledge through trips to Japan.

For a biography of Alfred Parsons, please refer to *Chris Beetles Summer Show*, 2016, pages 21-22.

62 (left)
Yellow Leaves
'When yellow leaves, or none, or few do hang'
Signed and inscribed with title below mount
Signed on reverse
Ink
7 ½ x 4 inches
Exhibited: Preliminary drawing for 'Yellow Leaves', Royal Academy Summer Exhibition, London, 1879, no 417

63 (opposite)
The Road to the Farm
Signed and dated 1881
Signed, inscribed with title and 'meadows by the Kennet – a sunny afternoon in early autumn' below mount
Ink
5 ½ x 9 ¼ inches
Exhibited: Preliminary drawing for 'The Road to the Farm',
Royal Academy Summer Exhibition, London, 1881, no 301

The Road to the Farm

This photo of Alfred Parsons in his studio shows him painting, or applying the finishing touches to 'The Road to the Farm'. The painting was exhibited in the Royal Academy Summer Exhibition in 1881, no 301.

This preliminary drawing in ink for the much larger oil painting is characteristic of Alfred Parson's working process. From his detailed outlines, you see the development of light and depth.

64
**Autumn in Japan
The Edge of
the Tokaido,
near Hamamatsu**
Signed
Inscribed with title
below mount
Ink with bodycolour
6 ¾ x 9 ¼ inches
Illustrated: Alfred Parsons,
Notes In Japan, New York:
Harper & Brothers
Publishers, 1896,
page 155

65
**White Azalea Bush
Raku-Raku-Tei,
Hikone**
Signed
Inscribed with title and
'Notes in Japan II' below
mount
Watercolour
8 x 10 ½ inches
Illustrated: Alfred Parsons,
Notes In Japan, New York:
Harper & Brothers
Publishers, 1896, page 69

66
Hemp Agrimony, Japan
Signed with initials and dated 1869
Watercolour
6 ¼ x 4 ½ inches

Hemp Agrimony, Japan

Hemp Agrimony is a plant native to Japan. It flourishes at the edges of rivers and ponds, and flowers toward the end of summer. It is known for being an excellent attractor for pollinators such as butterflies, as Alfred Parsons has depicted in this picture. In William Robinson's book *The Wild Garden*, illustrated by Alfred Parsons, they are described as:

'Vigorous perennials, with white or purple fringed flowers. Some of the American kinds might well be associated with our own wild one – the white kinds, like aromaticum and ageratoides, being very beautiful and distinct, and well worthy of a place in the best parts of the wild garden.'

William Robinson, *The Wild Garden*,
London: John Murray, 1883, page 137

ALFRED PARSONS

In *Notes in Japan*, the *Platycodon Grandiflorum* is also referred to by Alfred Parsons as a purple-blue campanula. He comes across it several times while in Japan, notably growing on the slopes near Yoshida.

The work by Totosha Harris [69] includes it as one of 'The Seven Beautiful Flowers of Late Summer', as number six – 'Kiku'.

The Latin name for this wildflower is *Corydalis Decumbens*. It flowers in forests and fields throughout April and is native to Japan. Here Alfred Parsons refers to its Japanese name, in full 'Jirobo-engosaku'. In the Ise province of Japan, 'Jiro-bo' means the second son in a family. They refer to the Viola as 'Taro-bo', or first son in a family, as they are the two most prevalent flowers in the region.

67
Platycodon Grandiflorum, "Kikyo"
Signed with monogram and inscribed with title
Inscribed 'notes in Japan IV' below mount
Ink
7 x 4 inches
Illustrated: Alfred Parsons, *Notes In Japan*, New York: Harper & Brothers Publishers, 1896, page 80;
Harper's New Monthly Magazine, December 1894, page 53, 'The Time of the Lotus' by Alfred Parsons

68
A Spring Flower – Jiro-Bo
Signed with monogram and inscribed 'a spring flower' and 'Notes in Japan I'
Ink
8 x 5 ½ inches
Illustrated: Alfred Parsons, *Notes In Japan*, New York: Harper & Brothers Publishers, 1896, page 78

TOTOSHA HARRIS

'I was walking one day at Yoshida with a Japanese artist, a remarkable man who was engaged in making a series of steel-engravings, half landscape and half map, of the country round Fuji, and called his attention to a splendid clump of pink belladonna lilies growing near an old gray tomb; but he would not have them at all, said they were foolish flowers, and the only reason he gave me for not liking them was because they came up without any leaves. When we got back to our tea-house he took my pen and paper, and showed me what were the seven beautiful flowers of late summer — the convolvulus, the name of which in Japanese is "asago," meaning the same as our "morning-glory"; wild chrysanthemum; yellow valerian; the lespedeza, a kind of bush clover; Platycodon grandi' florum, a purple-blue campanula; Eidalia japonica, the tall grass which covers so many of the hills; and shion, a rather insignificant-flowered aster.'

Harper's New Monthly Magazine, December 1894, pages 51-52, 'The Time of the Lotus' by Alfred Parsons

69
The Seven Beautiful Flowers of Late Summer
Signed and inscribed with title
Signed, inscribed with title and 'Notes in Japan IV' below mount
Ink
5 x 7 ¾ inches
Illustrated: Alfred Parsons, *Notes In Japan*, New York: Harper & Brothers Publishers, 1896, page 85;
Harper's New Monthly Magazine, December 1894, page 52, 'The Time of the Lotus' by Alfred Parsons

HECTOR CAFFIERI

Hector Edward Philippe Caffieri,
RBA RI ROI (1847-1931)

Though he is best known for his sensitive, atmospheric studies of fisherfolk – in ports that include his adopted home of Boulogne – Hector Caffieri was a wide-ranging painter of landscapes and genre scenes in the tradition of French academic naturalism.

For a biography of Hector Caffieri, please refer to *Chris Beetles Summer Show*, 2021, page 111.

70
A Quiet Afternoon, Poole Harbour
Signed
Watercolour with bodycolour
25 ½ x 41 inches
Provenance: The Howard Collection of Pictures. Sold by Leonard Joel, 362 Little Collins Street, Melbourne, 17th November 1942. Cat no 9 (Under Instructions From The Union Trustee Co of Australia Ltd and Peter Mccallum Esq)
Exhibited: Heatherley's School of Art Centenary Exhibition, London, 1996, no 51

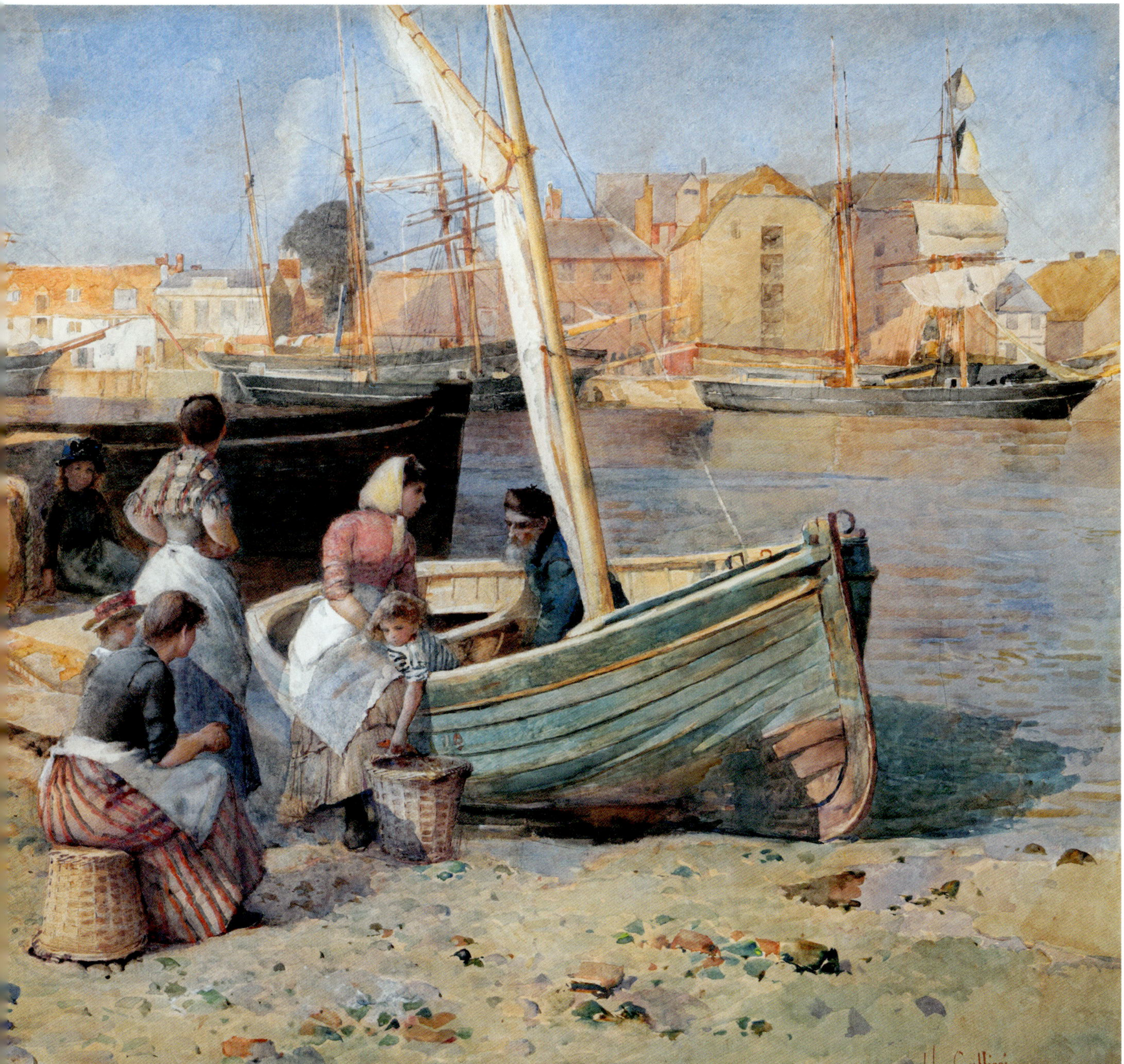
H. Caffieri.

CARLTON ALFRED SMITH

Carlton Alfred Smith, RBA RI ROI (1853-1946)

Carlton Alfred Smith was a painter, mainly in watercolour, of gentle rural genre scenes, including many of mothers and daughters.

For a biography of Carlton Alfred Smith, please refer to *Chris Beetles Summer Show*, 2020, page 119.

71
Girl with her Knitting
Signed and dated 1886
Watercolour
14 x 10 inches
Possibly the painting exhibited at the Royal Society of British Artists, Annual Exhibition, London, 1886-1887, no 568

72
After Sunday Church, 1888
(opposite)
Signed and dated 1888
Watercolour
28 ¼ x 19 ½ inches

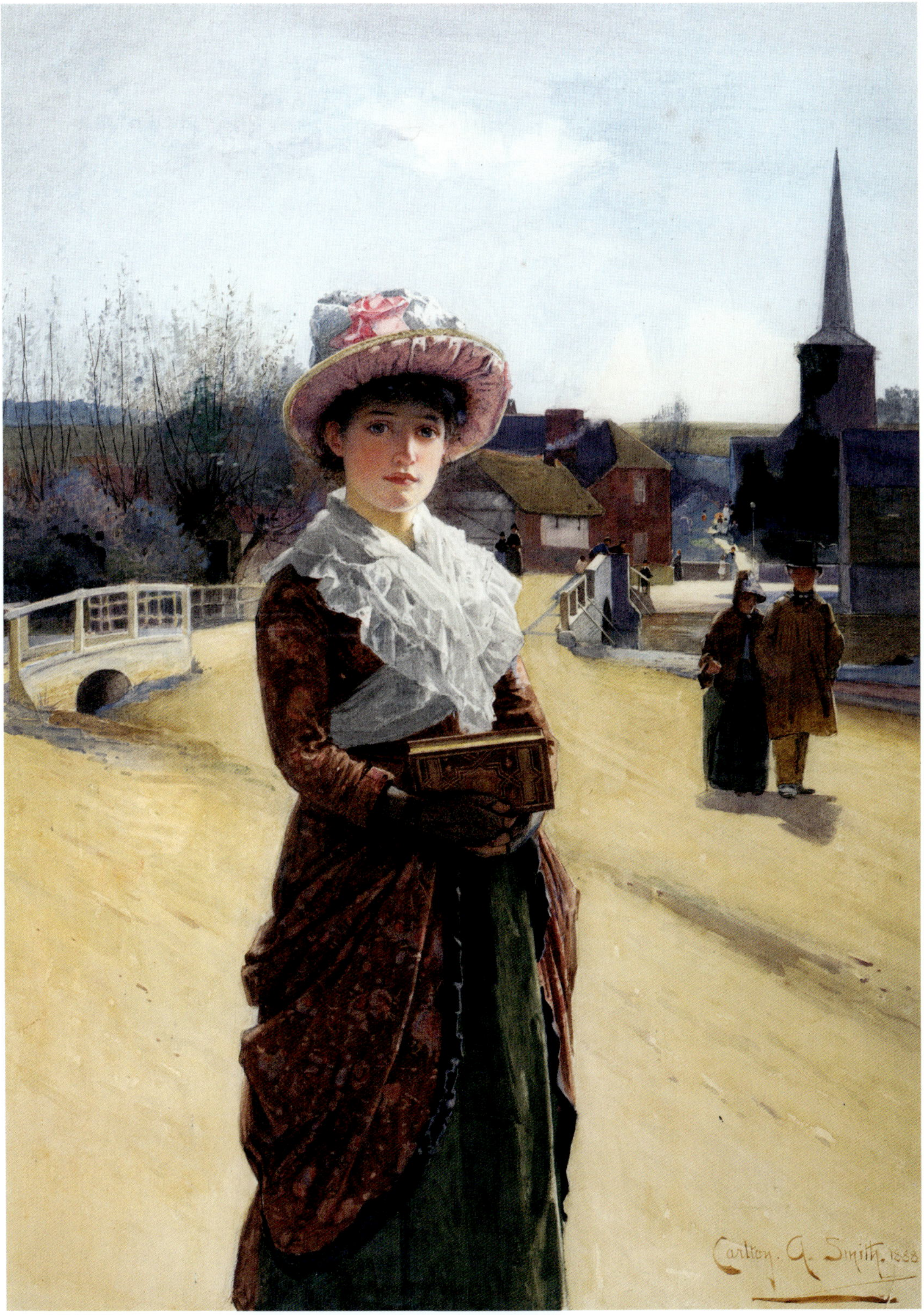
Carlton. A. Smith. 1888

CHARLES EDWARD WILSON

Charles Edward Wilson (1853–1941)

Charles Edward Wilson was a British watercolourist known for his sensitive depictions of rural life and childhood scenes. Born at Whitwell, Derbyshire, he was the son of the village schoolmaster and showed artistic promise from an early age. He trained at the Sheffield School of Art, where he developed the technical and observational skills that would characterise his mature work.

Later in life, Wilson settled in Witley, Surrey, where the surrounding countryside provided an inspirational subject matter. His watercolours typically focused on the everyday activities of countryside figures especially women and children, accompanied with careful draughtsmanship, a lightness of touch and detail, and a sense of nostalgia. His palette was delicate yet vivid, and his compositions were praised for their rhythmic design and graceful line.

He first exhibited at the Royal Academy in 1891, submitting a work entitled *Sweet Content*, and went on to contribute seventeen works there, as well as thirteen to the New Watercolour Society. He also exhibited at the Walker Art Gallery, Liverpool, among other notable venues. His reputation grew steadily during the late nineteenth and early twentieth centuries, with his images frequently reproduced on postcards and posters to meet public demand. Wilson often repeated the figures in the compositions of his paintings almost creating a narrative, using his neighbours as models. It was said that the magpie that so often appears in his paintings, was reared by him and after it died he had it stuffed by a taxidermist so he could continue to paint it.

Charles Edward Wilson moved within a wide artistic circle that included David Burliuk, a pioneer of the Russian avant-garde, Marc Chagall, celebrated for his dreamlike imagery, Albert Goodwin, known for his visionary landscapes, as well as Helen Allingham, whose depictions of English cottages and gardens closely aligned with his own subject matter. Most significantly however, he was a very close friend with Carlton Alfred Smith, with whom he shared a studio at Smith's House in Haverstock Hill near Hampstead before moving to Surrey. They often used the same models. Though his style remained rooted in the British tradition of rural genre painting, these associations reflect his awareness of broader artistic movements.

His work is represented in public collections including the Victoria and Albert Museum, and he remains regarded as one of the foremost exponents of sentimental watercolour painting in the Edwardian era.

73
Good News in the Post
Signed
Watercolour
21 ½ x 14 ¾ inches
Possibly the painting exhibited at the Royal Academy Summer Exhibition, London, 1917, no 783

71

WILLIAM HATHERELL

William Hatherell, (1855-1928)

William Hatherell was born at Westbury-on-Trym, near Bristol on 18 October 1855, and was educated at private schools. He worked in the City of London before studying art, from 1877, at the Royal Academy Schools and, under Fred Brown, at Westminster School of Art. Beginning his career as a painter, he showed work at the Royal Academy from 1879, and became a member of several exhibiting societies: the Royal Institute of Painters in Water-Colours (1888), the Royal Institute of Painters in Oils (1898), the Royal West of England Academy (1903) and the Royal British Colonial Society of Artists.

From the late 1880s, Hatherell increasingly applied his skills as a painter to his commissions as an illustrator, the new photographic methods of reproduction enabling him to work in oil on board as well as watercolour and pen and ink. He gained a reputation for refusing to produce hasty results, and became particularly expert in representing historical and literary subjects. Living in London, he joined the staff of the *Graphic* in 1892, contributed to other periodicals, and illustrated books.

He became equally popular in the United States, where his work appeared most notably in *Harper's New Monthly Magazine* and an edition of Mark Twain's *The Prince and the Pauper* (1909). His illustrative achievements led to his election as an honorary member of the Langham Sketching Club and a corresponding member of the American Society of Illustrators. He died in London on 7 December 1928.

His work is represented in the collections of the Victoria and Albert Museum, and Birmingham Museum and Art Gallery.

74
God Rest You Merry Gentlemen
Signed
Watercolour
11 ¾ x 6 inches

WALTER TYNDALE

Walter Frederick Roope Tyndale, RBC RI (1855-1943)

Walter Tyndale was one of the most popular and influential topographical watercolourists working at the turn of the century. He was also one of the first to benefit from the printing revolution of 1901 when his publishers, A & C Black, pioneered the use of three colour half-tone plates. The ensuing publishing boom led to a wealth of commissions for Tyndale for illustrated travel books, which took him from the Wessex countryside to Europe and the Far East.

For a biography of Walter Tyndale, please refer to *Chris Beetles Summer Show*, 2021, page 112.

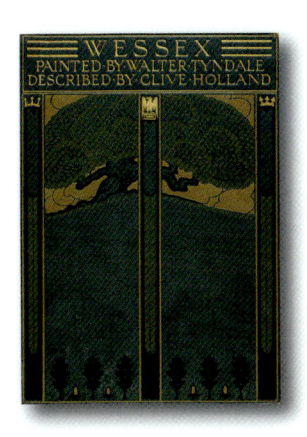

Clive Holland, *Wessex*, London: A & C Black, 1906

75
Bath Abbey
Signed
Inscribed with title on backboard
Watercolour
8 ¾ x 11 inches
Illustrated: Clive Holland, *Wessex*, London: A & C Black, 1906, plate 52
Exhibited: 'An Exhibition of Water-Colours of Wessex (Thomas Hardy's Country), by Walter Tyndale', Leicester Galleries, London, June-July 1905, no 24

HENRY HERBERT LA THANGUE

Henry Herbert La Thangue,
RA ROI NEAC (1859-1929)

Through his rustic genre scenes and landscapes, Henry Herbert La Thangue became a leading exponent of the British approach to Impressionism at the turn of the century.

For a biography of Henry Herbert La Thangue, please refer to *Chris Beetles Summer Show*, 2010, page 38.

76
A Spanish Mill
Signed
Oil on canvas
37 ¾ x 42 ½ inches

A Spanish Mill

Henry La Thangue was a founder member of the New English Art Club and like many of his fellow artists spent time painting in mainland Europe. He is most associated with Provence and the Liguria coast of Italy. He also sailed down the coast of Spain as far as Andalusia and the Balearic Islands.

He worked almost exclusively on the spot, and it is likely that he sketched the present composition by the roadside in the Mallorcan hills, close to the village of Buger. The fast-flowing Torrent de Buger irrigated the cereal crops produced in the area, giving rise to the construction of windmills hundreds of years earlier. At least one other work, the smaller *Moonrise in Spain* (Christie's, 16 December 2009), is known to have been completed at this location. The figure with the heavily laden donkey is a miller setting off for the coast or the local bake-house. Even into the 1920s, when the islands were colonised by artists such as Robert Graves, the native Spanish population continued to depend on the corn production of the small island.

ETHEL ATCHERLEY

Ethel Atcherley (1864-1905)

Known primarily as a landscape artist, depicting rustic scenes in watercolour and oil, Ethel Atcherley was also a talented sculptor, exhibiting work in this medium in her native Manchester. Before her premature death at the age of 41, she saw her works displayed at the Royal Academy of Arts, Manchester Academy of Fine Arts and the Royal Society of British Artists.

For a biography of Ethel Atcherley, please refer to *Chris Beetles Summer Show*, 2024, page 142.

77
The Harvesters
Signed
Watercolour with bodycolour
29 ¼ x 49 ¼ inches

ARTHUR REGINALD SMITH

Arthur Reginald Smith, ARA RSW RWS (1871-1934)

Most associated with his fresh and silvery watercolours of his native Yorkshire and, more generally, of northern England, Arthur Reginald Smith captured the rich landscapes of the United Kingdom.

For a biography of Arthur Reginald Smith, please refer to *Chris Beetles Summer Show*, 2017, page 95.

78
The Winding Road, Upper Wharfedale
Signed
Signed and inscribed with title on reverse
Watercolour
11 x 15 ½ inches
Provenance: Hon. Maude Lawrence, Ickenham Hall, Uxbridge

79
Town End, Cracoe
Signed
Watercolour with pencil
8 ¼ x 12 ¼ inches

80
Kilnsey, Yorkshire
Signed
Watercolour
10 x 9 ½ inches
Literature: Similar to 'Kilnsey', Halliwell Sutcliffe, *Striding Dales*, London: Frederick Warne & Co, 1927, plate 12

BEATRICE PARSONS

Beatrice Parsons (1869-1955)

Beatrice Parsons specialised in detailed representations of gardens, and especially floral borders. The results were exhibited in a large number of highly successful solo shows in London, and used to illustrate many books.

For a biography of Beatrice Parsons, please refer to *Chris Beetles Summer Show,* 2000, page 27.

81
Rhododendron and Bluebells, Oxhey Grange
Inscribed with title on reverse
Watercolour
9 x 12 inches

GERALD ACKERMANN

Gerald Ackermann (1876-1960)

Arthur Gerald Ackermann was a British watercolour painter, born on 13 February 1876 in Blackheath, London. Through his father's side, the family business was in art dealing. *Ackermann's* was a prominent gallery across central London that had been founded by Gerald Ackermann's grandfather Rudolph in 1792. His father Arthur Ackermann had inherited the business.

Gerald Ackermann's early art education was comprehensive, studying at the New College in Eastbourne as well as Heatherley's and Westminster School of Art in London. Between 1896 and 1901 he was a student at the Royal Academy Schools, where he won the Creswick Prize in 1900 and was also awarded the Landseer Scholarship.

During World War I, Gerald Ackermann enlisted in the Artists Rifles amongst many of his artistic contemporaries and by 1917 he was a part of the Army Education Corps.

Between 1893 and 1954 Gerald Ackermann exhibited his works annually at the Royal Academy Summer Exhibition. He was elected to the Royal Institute of Painters in Watercolours in 1912 and became a full member of the society in 1914. His solo shows included exhibitions at the Leicester Galleries and the Fine Art Society.

Gerald Ackermann found inspiration in nature and consistently looked to still life and the sweeping green landscapes of Great Britain. While his style is more typical of the 19th century than when he was actively painting, his subjects were drawn directly from his own surroundings. After settling in Blakeney in the 1930's his work favoured the countryside in which he lived, often featuring the Norfolk coast, town and landscape. He died nearby in Kelling.

82
The Road to the Downs
Signed
Watercolour with pencil
13 ¾ x 20 ¾ inches
Provenance: Royal Institute of Painters in Water Colours,
(Diploma work)
Exhibited: 'The Watercolour Tradition in Landscape',
Nunnington Hall, Yorkshire, April-June 2013

HAROLD SPEED

Harold Speed, RP (1872-1957)

Harold Edward Speed was born in London on 11 February 1872. His father was an architect, Edward Speed, and Harold was one of five sons.

In 1887 he began to study architecture at the Royal College of Art, but four years later moved to the Royal Academy to study painting. He received his first commission aged nineteen. In 1893 he was awarded a travel scholarship from the Academy. He then undertook a year-long painting tour of Europe, visiting many major cities such as Rome, Paris and Vienna. In his final year at the Royal Academy he painted the mural *Autumn*, which remains in the café of the Royal Academy to this day.

Upon graduating in 1896, Harold Speed was elected member of the Royal Society of Portrait Painters. It was in this area that he became renowned, and quickly earned commissions from London's elite. Around 1903 he was commissioned by Edward VII, after the King had seen his painting of a Maharajah and requested they meet at Buckingham Palace. The finished portrait was subsequently hung in the Royal Academy in 1905, and this was followed by his first solo-show at the Leicester Galleries in 1907.

Harold Speed was soon in constant demand, painting prominent politicians and nobility of the early 20th century. He exhibited widely across the United Kingdom with countless societies and artists groups. Further afield, he was elected an associate member of the Société Nationale des Beaux-Arts in Paris, and notably painted King Edward of Belgium in 1916.

Harold Speed also published practical handbooks for artists. These were *The Practice and Science of Drawing* (1913), *The Science and Practice of Oil Painting* (1924) and *What is the Good of Art?* (1936). He was elected as a Master of the Art Worker's Guild in 1916, and taught for many years at Goldsmith's College.

In 1920 he bought 23 Campden Hill Square, which had previously inspired the house in J M Barrie's first novel, *Peter and Wendy*. He converted the back of the house into a studio, and one of his lodgers following the First World War was the poet Siegfried Sassoon. In 1944, the property was damaged by a German doodle-bug bomb, and he spent the next eight years restoring the property and studio. He began to split his time between London and Oxford, while continuing to paint.

In 1953 Harold Speed first became unwell following a collapse at the Tate Gallery, which was he beginning of a prolonged illness. His wife Clara died on 11 June 1954, at their home in London. He spent most of the final years of his life at his home Court Meadow in Oxford, where he mainly painted landscapes. He described this as 'so much less pressing and exhausting than portraits…One needs immense stamina for the sittings of a portrait.'

Harold Speed died on 20 March 1957 in London. The Royal Watercolour Society held a retrospective exhibition of his work in 1959. His work is held in numerous public collections, including the National Portrait Gallery, Tate Gallery and V & A Museum.

83
Portrait of John Ellison McCartney Holding a Football
Signed and dated 1911
Oil on canvas
62 x 26 ½ inches
Provenance: The sitter and by descent to his Godson

The Ellison McCartneys were an Irish family whose seat was Clogher Park, County Tyrone. The Rt Hon Sir William Grey Ellison McCartney (1852-1924), possibly the sitter's father, was a governor of Western Australia.

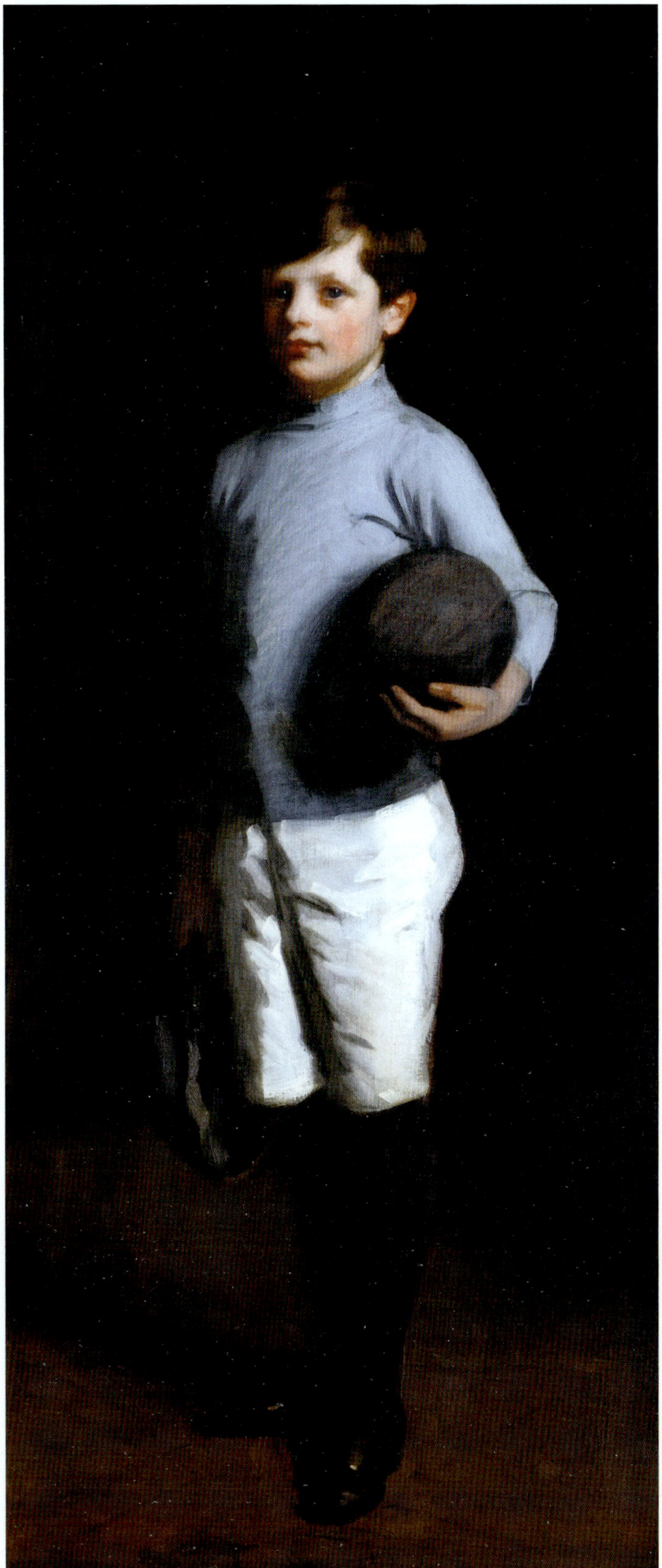

KATHARINE CAMERON

Katharine Cameron, FRSA RSW ARE (1874-1965)

Scottish artist, Katharine Cameron illustrated a number of memorable books for children, as well as producing distinctive paintings and prints of landscapes and flowers.

Katharine Cameron was born at Hillhead, Glasgow on 26 February 1874, the daughter of a United Presbyterian minister, and younger sister of the artist, David Young Cameron. She studied intermittently at Glasgow School of Art, under Fra Newbery, from 1889 to 1901, during which time she was a member of a group of female students who called themselves 'The Immortals'. In 1902, she went to Paris to study at the Académie Colarossi, under Gustave Courtois and R F-X Prinet. On her return, she lived with family members at Victoria Square, Stirling.

Between 1904 and 1910, she worked as a prolific illustrator of children's books for the Edinburgh publishers, T C & E C Jack, specialising in fairy stories and folk tales for their series, 'Told to the Children'. These included; *The Enchanted Land* (1906); *In Fairyland* (1910); *Celtic Tales* (1910). In 1908, Cameron travelled to Italy to prepare for one of her most important illustration works, for Amy Steed's *Legends and Stories of Italy for Children* (1909). On her return, she settled in Edinburgh, working from a studio in Forres Street. Cameron wrote and illustrated one book herself, *Iain the Happy Puppy: Being the Autobiography of a West Highland Terrier* (Moray Press, 1934).

Initially, her paintings and illustrations displayed the influence of the Glasgow School and its sources, while her etchings resembled and complemented those of her brother, D Y Cameron. The delicate style of her middle period was influenced by the landscapes of her brother, and of Joseph Crawhall junior and Edwin Alexander. However, she established herself at an early age as a distinctive talent. Indeed, as early as 1900, H C Marillier had devoted an article in the *Art Journal* to 'The Romantic Watercolours of Katharine Cameron'.

Cameron exhibited widely in Scotland and London, including the Royal Scottish Academy (from 1894) and Royal Academy (from 1921), and solo shows at the Scottish Gallery, Edinburgh (1913) and the Fine Art Society (1926). She was elected a member of the Glasgow Society of Lady Artists, the Royal Scottish Society of Painters in Watercolour (1897), the Scottish Society of Artists (1909) and an associate of the Royal Society of Painter-Etchers and Engravers (1920). She was living at Regent Terrace, Edinburgh, by 1921, and it remained her home following her marriage to the businessman and connoisseur, Arthur Kay, in 1928, at the age of 54. He died in 1939.

In the 1950s, Cameron became close to members of the Edinburgh Group, including William Gillies, and reverted to a more expressive compositional style. She was made a fellow of the Royal Scottish Academy in 1950, and of the Royal Society of Painter-Etchers and Engravers in 1964. She died at Marshall Crescent, Edinburgh, on 21 August 1965.

Her work is represented in numerous public collections, including the British Museum, Fleming Collection, Tate and the V&A; the National Galleries of Scotland (Edinburgh), Glasgow Museums and Aberdeen Art Gallery; and the Washington Library of Congress.

84 (opposite)
The Fairy Dance
Signed with initials
Watercolour and bodycolour with pencil
14 ¾ x 20 ¾ inches
Exhibited: 'The Illustrators. The British Art of Illustration 1780-1993', Chris Beetles Gallery, London, 1993, no 237

85 (right)
Over the dim blue hills
Signed
Signed, inscribed with title and dated 1908 on reverse
Watercolour
21 ¼ x 13 ½ inches

The title refers to the romantic poem, *Maire My Girl* by Irish poet John Keegan Casey. The poem celebrates Gaelic beauty and culture and reflects the romanticism and nationalism prevalent in both Ireland and Scotland at the turn of the 20th century.

> Over the dim blue hills
> Strays a wild river,
> Over the dim blue hills
> Rests my heart ever.
> Dearer and brighter than
> Jewels and pearl,
> Dwells she in beauty there,
> Maire my girl.
>
> [*first stanza*]

EDWARD STEEL HARPER

Edward Steel Harper, RBSA (1878-1951)

The work of the Birmingham artist, Edward Steel Harper, possesses a distinctive quality that combines late Pre-Raphaelitism with something more modern.

For a biography of Edward Steel Harper, please refer to *Chris Beetles Summer Show*, 2008, page 16.

His work is represented in numerous public collections, including Birmingham Museums & Art Gallery.

86
Bluebells and Gorse
Signed with monogram and dated 1914
Oil on canvas
11 ½ x 17 ½ inches

87
Island in the Loch
Signed with monogram and dated 1916
Oil on canvas
11 ½ x 17 ½ inches

88
April
Knightwick Worcs
Signed with monogram and dated 1935
Signed, inscribed with title and '946. 55 Moor Pool Avenue Harborne B'ham', and dated '30 Nov 1936' on label on reverse
Oil on board
19 ½ x 23 ¼ inches

GEORGE SHERINGHAM

George Sheringham, PS (1884-1937)

The versatile and eclectic artist, George Sheringham, found his forte when he became a designer of interiors and theatrical productions. In drawing on a deep knowledge of both western and eastern traditions, he created highly seductive worlds of fantasy.

George Sheringham was born in London on 13 November 1884, the elder son of the Rev Harry Alsager Sheringham, the then Vicar of St Peter's Westminster. Educated at the King's School, Gloucester, he studied under Henry Tonks at the Slade School of Art (1899-1901), and then under Harry Becker (1901-4). In 1904, he moved to Paris, and there developed his decorative style through visits to the collection of Eastern art at the Musée Guimet. Exhibiting at the Paris Salon, he may have held solo shows in 1905, in Paris and at the Ryder Gallery, London. While in France, he met and became engaged to Sybil Meugens (1877-1941), the daughter of an English accountant of Belgian descent, who was making her way as a painter. Returning to England in about 1907, he held a solo show in London's Brook Street Gallery in 1908, and then travelled in various parts of Europe and, most significantly, Algeria. At his debut as a decorative artist, at the Ryder Gallery in 1910, he exhibited silk panels that encouraged much interest and led to commissions to paint Chinoiserie panels for Judge Evans and Sir Albert Levy.

Following their marriage on 25 January 1912, George and Sybil Sheringham lived for a while with his family, in Northamptonshire and London, before moving to a house at Besant Cottage, 106 Frognal, Hampstead. They then shared their time between Frognal and Little Blenheim, Steeple Barton, Oxfordshire.

The Inspiration for the Dramas, the Operas and the Panels

The inspiration behind *The Cauldron of Annwn* was *The Mabinogion*, a collection of mediaeval Welsh manuscripts, mostly of the fourteenth century. First translated by Lady Charlotte Guest, and published between 1838 and 1849, the volumes comprise potent national mythology, including some early versions of Arthurian stories.

In turning to book illustration in 1915, with an edition of Max Beerbohm's *The Happy Hypocrite*, Sheringham made use of eighteenth-century imagery, which held him in good stead as a theatrical designer. His first set designs, for the Plough Club in 1917, foreshadowed long associations with the D'Oyly Carte Opera Company and Nigel Playfair at the Lyric Theatre, Hammersmith. Throughout the 1920s, he worked as both a theatrical and an interior designer, in Oriental and Baroque styles, a versatility that helped him win the Grand Prix at the Paris Salon in 1925. At the end of the decade, he accomplished his finest decorative scheme, for Eric Hamilton Rose at Leweston Manor, Dorset, by producing a number of murals based on the analysis of the rhythmic character of Oriental art. His achievements in interior decoration and textiles led him to be one of the first to be awarded the distinction of Royal Designer for Industry, in 1936. However, from 1932, ill health forced him to confine his movements, and in consequence he concentrated on still life painting. He exhibited a number of such subjects, in March 1937, in a solo show at the Fine Art Society. He died a few months later at his home in London on 11 November 1937. He had been a member of the Pastel Society and the London Sketch Club.

The Cauldron of Annwn

George Sheringham was commissioned to paint these large-scale watercolours on silk by Baron Howard de Walden as illustrations to *The Cauldron of Annwn*, his dramatic trilogy in verse. They represent two significant strands of late nineteenth and early twentieth-century creativity. Firstly, the choice of subject exemplifies the fascination of artists, composers and writers with ancient myths and their role in culture, as led by the paradigm of Richard Wagner. Secondly, the style epitomises a sophisticated Orientalist approach to decoration, influenced by the French, and applied by such British-based artists as Conder, Dulac and Ricketts to surfaces large and small. The combination of the Celtic and the Oriental in Sheringham's images suggest a parallel with those dramas of Yeats that present Irish myths through the form of Japanese Noh (dramas for which Dulac produced the designs). As such, they are a particularly fascinating contribution to European Symbolism.

89
The Cauldron of Annwn
(see following pages for individual cataloguing)

The Cauldron of Annwn

According to *The Mabinogion*, King Arthur descends to the underworld (Annwn) to retrieve a magical — and beautiful — cauldron of rebirth. This had the power to revive dead warriors slain in battle. The myth may be the origin of the Holy Grail, which was only later associated with the cup used by Jesus at the Last Supper.

In some Welsh traditions, Caerllan upon Usk (or Caerleon-on-Usk) was King Arthur's court, a few miles north of Newport. While Arthur sleeps, his knights tell tales. These knights include Kynon (or Cynan), son of Clydno Eiddyn. His tale – of a quest that leads to humiliation – inspires Owain to find the Lady of the Fountain.

89c

The Tale of Kynon, the son of Clydno when King Arthur was at Caerllan upon Usk
Signed
Watercolour with bodycolour and gold paint on silk
51 ½ x 19 ½ inches

89d
Playing music
Signed
Watercolour with bodycolour and gold paint on silk
58 x 22 ½ inches

'The Cauldron of the Head of Annwn: what is its faculty? Dark-blue and pearls around its rim It will not boil the food of a coward: it has not been so destined'

Branwen (or Bronwen, the eponymous character of the third part of *The Cauldron of Annwn*), is one of the Children of Llyr, the powers of darkness, but also the Welsh goddess of love and beauty. She marries Mathowlch, the King of Ireland, and takes with her the magical cauldron. Following mistreatment by her husband, war breaks out between the Irish and the British, and the British fair badly because they do not have the cauldron to rejuvenate them.

89e
Branwen
Signed
Watercolour with bodycolour and gold paint on silk
58 x 22 ½ inches

89f
Baptism of Dylan, Son of the Wave
Signed
Watercolour with bodycolour and gold paint on silk
22 ½ x 58 inches

Dylan (the eponymous character of the second part of *The Cauldron of Annwn*), is a son of Arianrhod and Gwydion, two of the Children of Don, the powers of light. However, Dylan himself is sometimes said to be a god of darkness as well as a sea god. Following his baptism by his great uncle, Math, the King of Gwynedd, he rushes into the sea and swims like a fish. When he returns to land, he is killed by an uncle, Gofannon, who does not know who he is.

STANLEY ANDERSON

Alfred Charles Stanley Anderson, RA RE (1884-1966)

The printmaker and painter, Stanley Anderson, was a major figure in the revival of line engraving between the wars. Though a long career allowed for a diverse range of subjects, his skill was displayed particularly well in a series of prints of farm workers and rural craftsmen.

For a biography of Stanley Anderson, please refer to *Chris Beetles Summer Show*, 2017, page 112.

90
Quai Duperre, La Rochelle
Signed and signed in plate
Inscribed with title and
'Edition 85 proofs' below mount
Etching
8 ¼ x 13 ¼ inches

91
The Haywain
Signed
Inscribed with title below mount
Watercolour
8 ¼ x 11 ½ inches

92
The Lane to the Hills
Signed
Inscribed with
title below mount
Watercolour
8 ½ x 11 ½ inches

93
The Road to Shillingford
Signed
Inscribed with
title below mount
Watercolour
8 ¼ x 11 ½ inches

94
Early Morning in September
Signed
Inscribed with title below mount
Watercolour
8 ½ x 11 ¾ inches
Exhibited: Royal Academy Summer Exhibition, London, 1950, no 894

95
Market Bound
Signed
Inscribed with title below mount
Watercolour
8 ½ x 12 inches
Exhibited: Royal Academy Summer Exhibition, London, 1945, no 982

96
Return to Pasture
Signed
Inscribed with title
below mount
Watercolour
9 x 12 ¾ inches

97
Loading Mangels
Signed and inscribed
'carting mangels' below mount
Watercolour
9 ½ x 12 ½ inches
Exhibited: Royal Academy
Summer Exhibition,
London, 1945

SNAFFLES

Charlie Johnson Payne (1884-1967), known as 'Snaffles'

Charlie Johnson Payne never received any formal artistic training but became one of the leading equestrian artists in the first half of the twentieth century. His work is noted for its accurate draughtsmanship and gentle humour; the latter a reflection of the kind and modest nature of the artist himself.

Christened Charlie, he was born in Leamington on 17 January 1884, the fourth of eight children of boot maker, Ambrose Johnson Payne. An artistic child, he formed, at an early age, not only a lifelong passion for drawing, but also the writings of Rudyard Kipling and a fascination with the military and all things equestrian. The latter he attributed to a schoolboy visit to the annual review of the Warwickshire Yeomanry on Warwick Common. At the outbreak of the Boer War and aged only fifteen, he tried to enlist, but he was clearly under age and rejected.

His fascination with the Army grew as did his interest in sketching and painting. At the age of 18 he joined the Royal Garrison Artillery and served three years as a Gunner. After leaving the army and despite having no formal training, he began to make a meagre living as an artist and to sign his work 'Snaffles'. From 1907, he submitted illustrations of hunting characters to the *Bystander* magazine and later to *The Illustrated Sporting and Dramatic News*. By the start of the First World War his artistic career had finally become established and his work was in demand.

In 1914, *The Graphic* sent him as part of a group of freelance artists to record the fighting on the Western Front. This work shows a stronger, more confident line and the accurate detailing for which he became well known. These wartime drawings and watercolours, were widely produced as prints, which were hand-coloured by Snaffles and his two sisters. After returning to England he enlisted in the Royal Naval Air Service, was later commissioned in the Royal Naval Volunteer Reserve and joined artist Norman Wilkinson's 'Dazzle' team, designing camouflage for the ships patrolling the North Atlantic.

In November 1915 Snaffles married Lucy Lewin, a marriage that would last for over half a century. After the end of the war he travelled abroad and in a series of very popular works (often humorous) recorded the life of the British Army in India, these included the sporting pastimes of polo and hunting and were sold at the Fores & Co Gallery in Piccadilly.

Returning to England, Snaffles's illustrations of hunting and country sports became increasingly sought after and he continued to contribute to many magazines including *Punch*.

At the beginning of the Second World War he helped design the camouflage of domestic airfields as well as joining the Home Guard. However, after their home, outside Guildford, narrowly missed a being bombed, he and his wife moved to Somerset. Tragically, at the end of the war, in 1945, a firework from the VE celebrations in Taunton destroyed the warehouse containing all of his pre-war sketchbooks, original paintings and prints.

After the war Snaffles and his wife settled in Tisbury in Wiltshire, where he continued to work from a studio, but his eyesight diminished and his artistic production sadly lessened. He died on 30 December 1967 at the age of eighty-three.

Wipers

This watercolour refers to one of the major and brutal battles fought in Ypres, West Flanders in 1914 during the First World War. 'Wipers' was the Tommy slang for the French city which was catastrophically damaged, the building behind the British soldier is the medieval Cloth Hall. This, the original watercolour, was reproduced as a contemporary print.

98
Wipers
Signed and inscribed with title
Watercolour with pencil
15 ½ x 9 inches

'Wipers'

CHARLES CUNDALL

Charles Cundall, RA RWS RP NEAC NS SMA (1890-1971)

Charles Cundall was born in Stretford, Lancashire on 6 September 1890. His first artistic training came as an apprentice at Pilkington's Pottery, designing pottery and stained glass under the Scottish designer Gordon Forsyth. In 1912, he studied at Manchester School of Art, before being awarded a scholarship to the Royal College of Art. However, his studies were interrupted in 1914 by the outbreak of the First World War. Serving in the Royal Fusiliers, Cundall was wounded in the right arm, forcing him to learn to paint with his left hand before returning to the RCA in 1918. He studied at the Slade School of Art from 1919 to 1920, before completing his education at the Académie Colarossi in Paris.

Following the completion of his studies, Charles Cundall travelled extensively, visiting Italy in 1921 and 1923, and also travelling to Sweden, Russia and Spain. The first solo show of his work was exhibited at Colnaghi's in Mayfair, London in 1927, followed by a number of exhibitions at leading London societies. He was elected to the New English Art Club (1924), the Royal Society of Portrait Painters (1933), the Royal Society of Painters in Water-Colours (ARWS 1935, RWS, 1941) and the Royal Academy (ARA 1937, ARA 1944).

At the start of the Second World War, Charles Cundall worked on a number of short-term contracts for the War Artists' Advisory Committee before being given a full-time salaried commission as an Admiralty artist to work on Merchant Navy subjects, working on the Thames, the Medway and in the West Country. In 1941, he was assigned to the Air Ministry, where he worked on Bomber Command and Coastal Command subjects. In 1943, he was commissioned to paint the commemoration ceremony for the Battle of Britain, before visiting Quebec in 1944. He died in London on 4 November 1971.

Collections of his work are held in the Imperial War Museum, the RAF Museum and Southampton City Art Gallery.

A Cup Tie

The subject of the this painting is the 1926 3rd round FA Cup tie between Corinthians and Manchester City, played at The Crystal Palace, the match ending in a 3-3 draw. The replay was held at Maine Road a week later, with Manchester City defeating Corinthians 4-1. Manchester City reach the final of this season's competition, losing 1-0 to Bolton Wanderers.

99
A Cup Tie At Crystal Palace, Corinthians V Manchester City
Signed
Inscribed with title and '1-3' and dated '9 January 1926'
on a label on reverse
Oil on panel
23 ¼ x 29 ¼ inches
Literature: I Bevan, S Hibberd and M Gilbert, *An Affectionate History of Football at the Crystal Palace, To The Palace For the Cup*,
London: Replay Publishing, 1999, pages 142-3

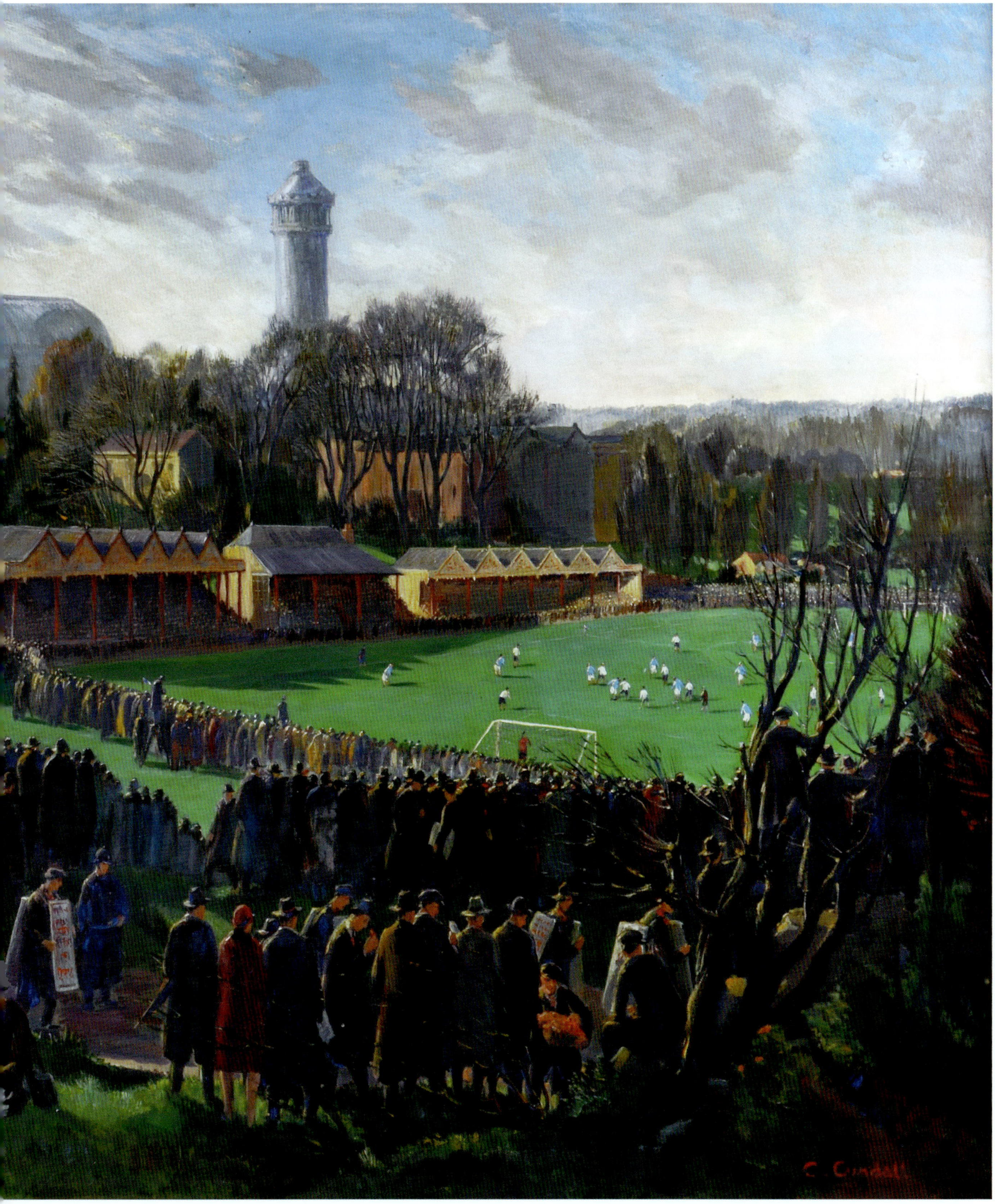

ALFRED REGINALD THOMSON

Alfred Reginald Thomson, RA (1894-1979)

Alfred Reginald Thomson was a multi-faceted artist who was highly sought-after as a commercial artist and portrait painter. Across his career, Thomson found success and critical acclaim designing iconic advertising campaigns for the LNER and painting portraits of sitters such as Alfred Hitchcock and the Duke of Edinburgh. He also distinguished himself as an Official War Artist in the RAF, and won a gold medal for painting at the 1948 London Olympics.

Alfred Reginald Thomson was born on 10 December 1894 in Bangalore, India, to George Thomson, a British Civil Engineer, and his Irish wife Florence (neé Green). Thomson was born deaf and on the family's return to England, he was enrolled at the age of seven at the Royal School for Deaf Children in Margate, where he learned sign language. After attending a private school in Brondesbury, north London, intended to help with his speech, he studied at the London Art School in Kensington, where he was tutored by C M Q Orchardson and John Hassall. However, Thomson failed to pass the exam for entry into the Royal Academy Schools, and instead was sent to work on a farm in Lenham, Kent, by his father, who strongly opposed his son pursuing a career in the arts. He soon returned to London and found work designing posters for a whisky company and later a series of posters for Daimler cars.

By the end of the First World War, Alfred Reginald Thomson was establishing himself as a commercial artist. In the interwar period, Thomson was commissioned to design advertising campaigns for companies such as Three Nuns Tobacco, Horlick's and, most famously, for the London & North Eastern Railway (LNER). He produced some of the LNER's most iconic posters during this time, including the 'Then and Now' campaign and 'Take me by the Flying Scotsman'. In 1922, he produced a series of murals, the 'Pickwick Panels', for the Duncannon Hotel, which were greatly acclaimed and were saved and transported to the United States when the hotel was demolished in 1930. In 1934, a series of murals Thomson produced for the Limmer & Trinidad Lake Asphalt Company were exhibited at Olympia, London. Thomson would also design murals for the Science Museum, London, the Palais de Danse, Derby, the Darlington Children's Library and Birmingham Dental Hospital. In 1953, he restored murals at the Saville Theatre, London, and added one of his own. For many years, he was commissioned to design the decorations for the annual Chelsea Arts Ball.

In addition to his work as a commercial artist, Alfred Reginald Thomson developed a reputation as a talented portrait painter. He exhibited regularly at the Royal Academy from 1920, became an associate member in 1938 and a full Royal Academician in 1945. Sitters for his portraits included Alfred Hitchcock (Royal Academy, 1933), Sir Charles Wheeler (Royal Academy, 1964) and the Duke of Edinburgh (Royal Academy, 1964).He became a member of the Royal Society of Portrait Painters in 1944.

During the Second World War, he completed a number of commissions for the War Artists' Advisory Committee. In September 1942, he took over from Eric Kennington as a full-time salaried War Artist attached to the Air Ministry, though he was later forced to resign after being wounded in an accidental shooting. In 1948, he represented Great Britain at the London Olympics, winning a gold medal for his painting of boxers at the London Amateur Boxing Championships. He would be the first and last British man to win an Olympic medal for painting before it was discontinued.

Later in his career, he was commissioned to paint a number of works at the Houses of Parliament. In 1960, he produced an oil painting of Prime Minister Harold Macmillan at the despatch box, and a large scale painting of the House of Lords in 1961. In May 1979, he painted from the public gallery as Margaret Thatcher spoke at the despatch box on her first day as Prime Minister. Titled *First Time at the Box*, the painting was unfinished by the time of Thomson's death on 27 October 1979 and was considered lost until its discovery at a garage sale in 2015.

100
Self Portrait
Signed
Oil on board
17 ½ x 14 ¾ inches

103

NORMAN HOWARD

Norman Douglas Howard, SMA (1899-1955)

Norman Howard was a painter of marine, transport and architectural subjects. He was particularly known for his poster designs which epitomise the novelty, excitement and availability of travel in the first half of the twentieth century.

Born on 13 April 1899, Howard studied at the Camberwell School of Art 1918-20 and then at the Westminster School of Art under Walter Bayes from 1920-24. He exhibited widely including at the Royal Academy, the Society of Aviation Artists (at their inaugural exhibition in 1954) and the Society of Marine Artists (he was elected a member in 1938). His many posters for the Railway companies and a large series of educational posters for Macmillan encompass such diverse subjects as railway journeys in Britain and Africa as well as industry and agriculture. Norman Howard lived in Richmond, Surrey, and died on 9 March 1955.

101
Kittyhawk 17 December 1903
Signed
Watercolour with bodycolour and pencil
10 ½ x 15 ½ inches
Exhibited: Society of Aviation Artists, 1954

Kittyhawk 17 December 1903

The Wright Flyer of 1903, was the first powered and manned aircraft to demonstrate sustained flight. Designed and built by Wilbur and Orville Wright in Dayton, Ohio, it was assembled in the autumn of 1903 at a camp on the isolated dunes near Kitty Hawk, North Carolina. The first attempt on 14 December failed, but the aircraft successfully flew four times on 17 December, covering distances of 120, 175, 200, and 852 feet respectively.

The Kitty Hawk's strong but flexibly braced biplane structure was made of a framework of spruce and ash covered with a fine muslin cloth and the two contra-rotating propellers were powered by a four cylinder petrol engine. The pilot (both Wilbur and Orville alternated) lay on the lower wing with his hips in a padded wooden cradle, the movement of his hips as well as a small hand lever regulated the pitch and yaw and gave limited control.

Sadly, after the fourth flight on 17 December, a sudden gust of wind badly damaged the Kitty Hawk and it was never flown again. It was repaired and in 1928 it went on display in the Science Museum, London. It remained there for 20 years and in 1948 it was transferred for permanent display at the Smithsonian Institution, Washington.

19TH CENTURY SCHOOL

The young girl in this portrait is likely to be Aileen Beatrice Woodroffe (1890-1985), who would have been aged 12 at the time it was painted. She lived with her parents and elder sister, Vera, in a large house in Kensington. During the First World War both sisters served as Army Volunteer Aid Detachments (VADs) in hospitals near the front line in France.

In later life she moved to Abbey House, Witchampton, Dorset. After Aileen's death, the contents, including this painting, were sold in a major house sale by Sotheby's on 19 May 1986. The Woodroffe sisters also bequeathed an impressive collection of art to eight British museums including the Fitzwilliam Museum, Cambridge and their letters, written as VADs during the First World War, are with the Imperial War Museum, London.

102
Young Girl with Shuttlecock
Signed with monogram and dated 02
Watercolour
15 ½ x 10 ¾ inches

EARLY 20TH CENTURY ENGLISH SCHOOL

George Frederic Watts at Limnerslease, November 1903

A label on the original backboard read, 'I bequeath this dear portrait of Signor to the artist and donor Mrs Alfred Southerby. Lennox Lodge, 54 Lennox Gardens'. G F Watts was known as 'Signor' to his closest friends.

George Frederic Watts OM, RA (1817-1904) was one of the most successful British artists of the 19th century. The drawing is based on a photograph reproduced in, Mary Seton Watts, *George Frederick Watts: the annals of an artist's life*, (1912, facing page 314). The photograph was titled, 'G F Watts at Limnerslease November 1903, an instantaneous photograph', and it was taken by Sir Emery Walker, an engraver, photographer and printer and part of the William Morris and Arts and Crafts movement.

In these last two years of his life, at the age of 87, Watts was spending more time in his home Limnerslease, Compton, Surrey and less in London, in an attempt to complete the larger than life sculpture of Lord Tennyson and his dog, Karenina for the City of Lincoln. The chalk drawing taken from this photograph shows a quiet, domestic moment. The two cups infer that Watts had company, either his loyal wife and indefatigable biographer, Mary, or his friend and photographer Sir Emery Walker.

There is some uncertainty as to the artist. The previous attribution, Mrs Alfred Southerby, a friend and amateur artist, appears increasingly unlikely. The artist could be his wife, Mary Watts, who was a talented and sensitive artist in her own right or even by George Frederic Watts himself, in the last months of his life. More research is needed.

103
George Frederic Watts at Limnerslease, November 1903
Coloured chalk
16 ½ x 21 inches

JESSIE DUNLOP

Jessie I Dunlop (1902-1970)

Though she is little known, Jessie Dunlop well represents the distinctive character of Scottish art in the early twentieth century.

Jessie Dunlop was from the Scottish town of Paisley, to the west of Glasgow. Studying at Glasgow School of Art, she developed as a painter in oil of portraits and figure groups, which she exhibited mainly at Paisley Art Institute, but also at the Aberdeen Artists Society and the Royal Scottish Academy (RSA).

While her portraits – of dogs as well as humans – tend to be naturalistic, her figure compositions are Symbolist in approach. They may be compared to the work of John Duncan and other artists of the Celtic Revival, but are more eclectic in style and wide ranging in theme, responding as they do to imagery and narrative that is variously Biblical, Classical and Oriental.

The eclecticism of the present work, in which Dawn drives an astrological procession, can be seen particularly in the representation of the earth: Islamic buildings combining with Celtic vegetal knots.

While exhibiting this work, at the RSA in 1934, Dunlop was living at 'Lathan Sona', Kinpurnie Road, Paisley, though she sent it from Slapton, near Kingsbridge, Devon, where she was probably on holiday. The original frame was produced by Glasgow maker, John Gibson. Two years later, she moved to the west coast town of Largs, in Ayrshire. At some point, she painted R B McPhaden, who had been Provost (or Mayor) of Largs in the years 1928-30.

104
Dawn
Signed
Oil on canvas laid down on board
25 x 37 inches
Exhibited: Royal Scottish Academy, Edinburgh 1934, no 556

MICHAEL BERNARD CRITCHLOW

Michael Bernard Critchlow (1904-1972)

Michael Bernard Critchlow was born Bernard Critchlow Green on 21 June 1904 in Wolverhampton. He studied at Wolverhampton School of Art under Robert Jackson Emerson, before becoming a freelance illustrator in the 1930s. After the Second World War, he was commissioned to design a number of posters for the Ministry of Information, and produced illustrations for publications including *The Strand*, *Britannia and Eve*, *John Bull* and *Woman's Own*. In 1948, he was selected to represent Great Britain in painting at the Summer Olympics in London. The gold medal was won by Alfred Reginald Thomson (see page 102). Throughout his career, he was known as 'Jerry' Critchlow, and in addition to his work as an illustrator, produced oils that were exhibited at the Royal Academy, Royal Society of Portrait Painters, New English Art Club and Royal Institute of Oil Painters.

Michael Bernard Critchlow lived much of his life in London, but also spent periods living in Berkhamsted, Hertfordshire, and Brixham, Devon. He developed Parkinson's later in life, and died in Hammersmith on 29 September 1972. He was survived by his wife Rosalind (neé Weston Mann), whom he had married on 29 September 1930, and their son Keith (born 1933), who would become a successful artist, professor of architecture and leading expert in sacred geometry.

105
Craven Cottage
Signed and dated '53
Oil on canvas board
36 x 24 inches
Exhibited: 'Football and the Fine Arts',
the Football Association,
Park Lane House, London,
October-November 1953, no 16

S R BADMIN

Stanley Roy Badmin, RWS RE AIA FSIA (1906-1989)

Throughout his career, S R Badmin used his great talents – as etcher, illustrator and watercolourist – to promote a vision of the English countryside and thus of England itself. By underpinning his idealism with almost documentary precision and detail, he was able to produce images that appealed to all, and could be used for a great variety of purposes, from education through to advertising.

The wellbeing suggested by each rural panorama is all the more potent, and pleasing, for the accuracy of each tree and leaf, and the plausibility of the slightest anecdotal episode.

For a biography of Stanley Roy Badmin, please refer to *Chris Beetles Summer Show*, 2017, page 124.

106
Study For 'Polstead', Early Spring 1935
Signed with initials, inscribed with title and dated 1935
Watercolour with ink
8 x 10 inches
Exhibited: Royal Society of Painters in Water-Colours, London, Autumn 1978, no 69

'The River Dee flows down from the central mass of the Grampian Mountains into the North Sea, and the upper reaches of the river yield many colourful views of mixed mountain and valley scenery. It is called Royal Deeside because of the King's Scottish home at Balmoral, but downstream from Braemar there are also numerous Scottish baronial seats such as that shown in the middle distance. Dominant features of this Scottish landscape are the conifers which clothe the mountain sides, and the narrow strip of cultivated land flanking the meandering river. In the background the distant mountains show their characteristic blue tinge, the highest one of all capped with a patch of snow. Though there are no permanent snowfields in the Grampians, only in the hottest summers does all the snow disappear.'

Park Browman et al, *The British Countryside in Colour*, page 144

107
The River Dee from Creag Choinnich
Signed
Inscribed 'R.Dee from Craig Choinnich' and dated 1948 below mount
Watercolour with ink
9 ¼ x 11 ½ inches
Illustrated: Park Browman et al, *The British Countryside in Colour*,
London: Odhams Press, 1951, facing page 144, as 'On Deeside'

108
Trees at the Castle Entrance
Signed
Signed with initials, inscribed 'Lime Trees, Faces at the Castle Gate, Arundel'
and dated 1971-2 below mount
Watercolour
11 x 8 inches
Exhibited: Royal Society of Painters in Water-Colours, London, Autumn 1972, no 137;
'Society of Sussex Painters, Sculptors and Engravers', Worthing Art Gallery, 1972,
no 74 as 'Two Trees at the Castle Entrance'

109 (above)
The Deserted Station, Fittleworth
Signed, inscribed 'Fittleworth Station Line Crossing'
and dated 'May 1966'
Watercolour
5 ¼ x 8 ¼ inches
Exhibited: 'S R Badmin, RWS, RE, ARCA, FSIA', Worthing
Art Gallery, November-December 1967, no 102;
'S R Badmin RWS', Chris Beetles Gallery, London,
June 1985, no 44

110 (below)
Four Wents Near Goudhurst, Kent
Signed and inscribed with title
Watercolour
4 ¼ x 8 ½ inches
Possibly the work exhibited at Royal Society
of Painters in Water-Colours, London, Autumn 1974,
no 136 as 'Oast Houses near Goudhurst'

111
The Upper Reaches of the River Severn
Signed twice
Signed with initials and inscribed 'The Upper Severn sun glitter
on water but soft grey cloud hills bluish from the Oswestry-Welshpool
rd near Buttingdon? 1956-1973.' on reverse
Watercolour and bodycolour
8 ½ x 12 ¾ inches
Provenance: Anthony Wylam Collection
Exhibited: Royal Society of Painters in Water-Colours, Autumn 1973, no 49;
'Society of Sussex Painters, Sculptors and Engravers', Worthing Art Gallery, November 1973

MERVYN PEAKE

Mervyn Peake (1911-1968)

Though already developing as a painter, Mervyn Peake established himself as a writer and illustrator in 1939, with *Captain Slaughterboard Drops Anchor*, a comic fantasy intended for children. This revealed that he had an outstanding talent for the grotesque, and was ready to align himself to Romantic tendencies in British art. He applied that talent to a broad range of visual and verbal forms, central to which was his 'Gormenghast' trilogy, an extraordinary imaginative achievement detailing a parallel world.

Mervyn Peake was born on 11 July 1911 in Kuling, Central Southern China, the summer residence of his father. He was the younger son of the missionary doctor, Ernest Cromwell Peake, and his wife, Amanda (née Powell), a missionary nurse. In the calm following the Communist Revolution, the Peake family settled in Tientsin (now Tianjin), close to Peking. Apart from a sojourn in England during the First World War, Peake spent all his early years there, so that its landscape and way of life retained a strong hold on his imagination.

In 1923, the family finally settled permanently in England, and Mervyn attended Eltham College, Kent, where he excelled at drawing. He then studied at Croydon School of Art (1929) and the Royal Academy Schools (1929-32), where he won the Arthur Hacker Prize (1930). While still a student, he exhibited for his one and only time at the Royal Academy (1931). He then joined an artists' colony on the Channel Island of Sark, in order to write and paint. He exhibited with the group on the island and, in 1934, in London at the Cooling Galleries.

On his return to England in 1935, Peake spent three years as a part-time teacher at the Westminster School of Art; while there, he held his first solo show, at the Calmann Gallery (March 1937), and married a student of the art school, the painter, Maeve Gilmore (in December of the same year). Their three children – Sebastian, Fabian and Clare – would appear frequently in his drawings.

In 1939, Peake published his first book *Captain Slaughterboard Drops Anchor*, an illustrated comic fantasy. This revealed him as an illustrator with an outstanding talent for the grotesque, ready to align himself to Romantic tendencies in British art.

While serving in the army, from 1940, Peake concentrated less on painting than on writing and illustrating, and began to work on *Titus Groan*, the first novel of his famous Gormenghast trilogy. Following his discharge as an invalid, in 1943, he completed the novel and published his acclaimed illustrations to *The Rime of the Ancient Mariner* (1943). He was soon considered 'the greatest living illustrator' (John Watney, *Mervyn Peake*, London: Michael Joseph, 1976, page 121). His illustrative projects from this time include *Witchcraft in England* by Christina Hole (1945) and *Dr Jekyll and Mr Hyde* (1948) and contributions to *Radio Times* and, of his own writings, *Rhymes without Reason* (1944) and *Titus Groan* (1946). In 1945, he also visited Germany for *Leader* magazine to record the war-time devastation, and made drawings at Belsen which profoundly affected his later work.

Peake then returned to Sark, with his family, for a period of three years (1946-49), during which he wrote the second volume, *Gormenghast*; published in 1950, it received both the Heinemann Award for Literature and a prize from the Royal Society of Literature in the following year. The final volume of the trilogy, *Titus Alone*, was published in 1959. Through the 1950s, he taught drawing at the Central School of Arts and Crafts. But, from the middle of the decade, he suffered from Parkinson's disease which made work increasingly difficult. He completed his illustrations to Balzac's *Droll Stories* (1961) and his own *The Rhyme of the Flying Bomb* (1962) only with his wife's help and encouragement. He died on 17 November 1968 after spending the last four years of his life in hospital.

His work is represented in numerous public collections, including the Imperial War Museum; and the Wordsworth Trust (Grasmere). The Mervyn Peake Archive, which includes original drawings, is held by the British Library.

Further reading:
John Batchelor, *Mervyn Peake. a biographical and critical exploration*, London: Duckworth, 1974;
Colin Manlove (rev Clare L Taylor), 'Peake, Mervyn Laurence (1911-1968)', in H C G Matthew and Brian Harrison (eds), *Oxford Dictionary of National Biography*, Oxford University Press, 2004, vol 43, pages 269-271;
John Watney, *Mervyn Peake*, London: Michael Joseph, 1976;
G Peter Winnington (ed), Mervyn Peake. *The Man and His Art*, London: Peter Owen Publishers, 2006;
G Peter Winnington, *Vast Alchemies. The Life and Work of Mervyn Peake*, London: Peter Owen Publishers, 2000;
Malcolm Yorke, *Mervyn Peake: My Eyes Mint Gold: A Life*, London: John Murray, 2000

112
Maeve Breastfeeding Sebastian
Signed
Watercolour and bodycolour on tinted paper
33 x 44 inches

NORMAN NEASOM

Norman Neasom, RWS RBSA SAS (1915-2010)

Having grown up on a farm in Worcestershire, Norman Neasom developed into a master of the figure in the landscape. However, he did so in a variety of ways, creating work that ranged from the purely naturalistic through the caricatural to the poetic and surreal, and that seemed to straddle the pagan and the pious.

For a biography of Norman Neasom, please refer to *Chris Beetles Summer Show*, 2015, page 55.

113
Cilgerran Castle
Signed and dated 1984
Signed, inscribed with title and dated 1984 on reverse
Watercolour and bodycolour
12 x 16 ¼ inches
Exhibited: Royal Society of Painters in Water-Colours, London

Neasom depicts the striking 13th century fortress, Cilgerran Castle, perched overlooking the spectacular Teifi Gorge. But, this dramatic landscape has his characteristically human touch, fishermen with their traditional coracles (cwrwgl) and tourists peering down from the vertiginous castle terrace above.

114
Nantgwynant
Home from Shopping
Signed and dated 1992
Signed, inscribed with title and dated 1992 on reverse
Watercolour
12 x 10 ¾ inches

115

Himbleton Church from Bow Brook
Signed and dated 1990
Signed, inscribed with title and dated 1990 on reverse
Watercolour and bodycolour
13 ½ x 11 ¼ inches
Exhibited: Royal Society of Painters in Water-Colours, London

BERNARD DUNSTAN

Andrew Harold Bernard Dunstan,
RA PRWA NEAC HPS (1920-2017)

Bernard Dunstan was brought up in the tradition of Degas, Sickert and Vuillard, and established himself with intimate figure subjects and landscapes in paint and pastel. A member of both the Royal Academy and the New English Art Club for many years, he was much loved and greatly respected.

For a biography of Bernard Dunstan, please refer to
Chris Beetles Summer Show, 2019, page 106.

116
Arsenal Scores
Oil on board
7 x 14 inches
Exhibited: 'Football and the Fine Arts', the Football Association, Park Lane House, London, October-November 1953, no 22

117
Wash Time
Signed with initials
Inscribed 5/55 on reverse
Oil on board
11 ¼ x 15 ½ inches

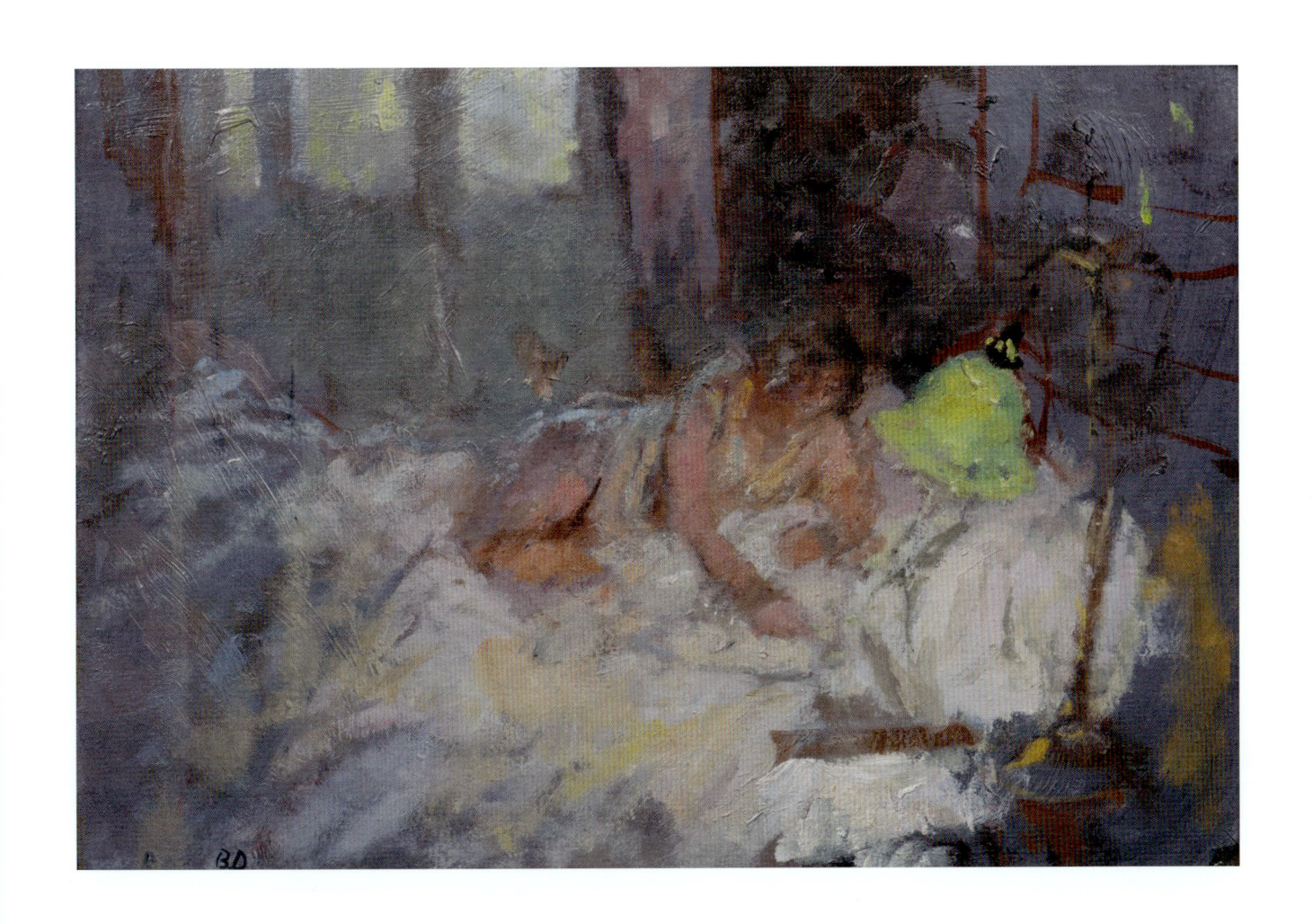

118
Morning Papers: The Green Lamp
Signed with initials
Inscribed with title and dated 7.04 on reverse
Oil on board
9 x 13 ¼ inches

PETER COKER

Peter Godfrey Coker, RA (1926-2004)

'One of the foremost realist painters in England ... Coker will be remembered for the refreshing nature of his astringent vision, for his consummate mastery as a draughtsman, painter and etcher, and as a proud and vigorous inheritor of a great artistic tradition.'

(Frances Spalding, *Independent*, 20 December 2004)

For a biography of Peter Coker, please refer to *Chris Beetles Summer Show*, 2015, page 48

Waves and Rock (opposite)

In 1957, Peter Coker passed his driving test and his first excursion abroad was with his wife and son, Vera and Nicholas, to stay at Le Corsaire in Étretat, Normandy and Hôtel de la Plage in Audierne, Brittany. As his second solo show at the Zwemmer Gallery approached he did some painting on site.

'The coasts of Normandy and Brittany called for the use of distinct palettes and techniques ... It is therefore not surprising that ... Waves and Rock should remain close in character to the earlier paintings of Étretat. Land and sea are again represented, respectively, in terms of solidity and power. Cliff and beach have a literal density, slabs of pigment recreating the geology from rock face to pebble; broader, more dynamic strokes enact the movement of the breakers. Yet the two not only meet – in depicting water on the shore – but are united in both their stress on pictorial surface and their deceptively restricted range of colour.'

Peter Coker RA, 2002, pages 57 and 59

119 (below)
Mouthier-Haute-Pierre, Jura
Signed with initials
Signed and inscribed 'Mouthier Jura. Mouthier Haute Pierre' on reverse
Oil on board
10 x 15 ¼ inches
Provenance: Mr Safier
Literature: *Peter Coker RA*, London: Chris Beetles, 2002, pages 130 and 151, Catalogue Raisonné no 342
Exhibited: Royal Academy Summer Exhibition, London, 1977, no 243

Probably painted at the beginning of October 1973 on Peter's second visit to the Jura within the same year.

120 (opposite)
Waves and Rock
Signed
Signed, inscribed with title, 'No 1' and artist's address on reverse
Oil on board
48 x 32 inches
Literature: *Royal Academy Illustrated*, 1964, page 17;
Peter Coker RA, London: Chris Beetles, 2002, pages 57, 59, 119 and 146, Catalogue Raisonné no 55
Exhibited: Zwemmer Gallery, London, October-November 1957, no 11;
Royal Academy Summer Exhibition, London, 1964, no 82;
Sheffield Art Galleries

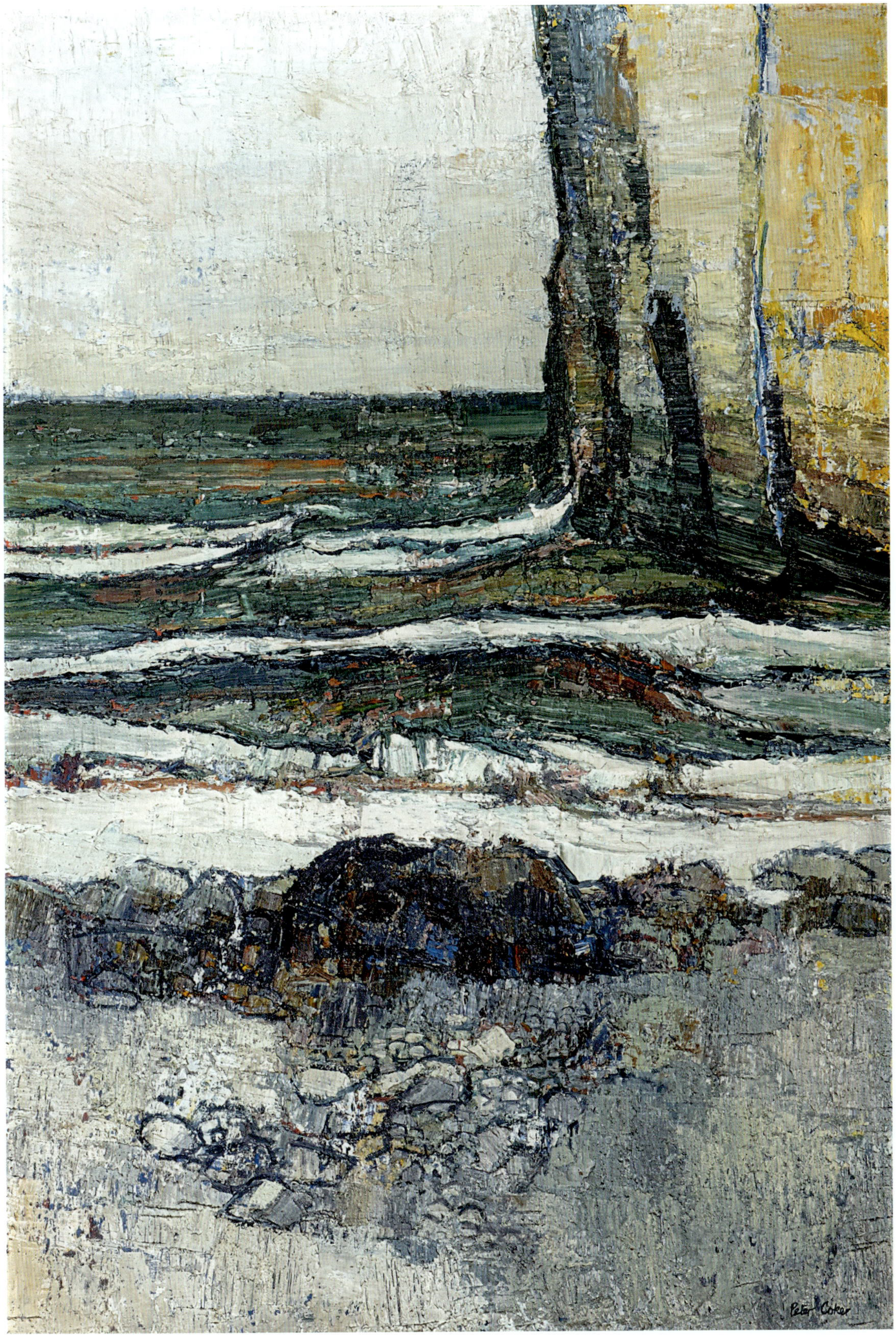
Peter Coker

121
Landscape Le Muy
Signed with initials
Signed and dated 'Aug 1979' on reverse
Oil on canvas
18 x 24 inches
Provenance: Mr and Mrs M Culucundis
Literature: *Peter Coker RA*, London: Chris Beetles, 2002, pages 133 and 153, Catalogue Raisonné no 402
Exhibited: 'Peter Coker', Gallery 10, London, November-December 1980, no 16

Two paintings of this title were exhibited at Peter Coker's 1980 solo exhibition at Gallery 10, but this painting, the larger of the two, was no 16.

Painted after one of two trips he made in 1979 to Bargemon, in south eastern France. Le Muy is half a hour south of Bargemon and the painting depicts the view south from Le Muy, of the river Argens.

122
Cleaning Nets, Quiberville
Signed
Signed, inscribed with title and dated 1989 on reverse
Inscribed with title, medium and dimensions in inches and 'cat no 127' on label on reverse
Inscribed 'no 356' and dated 1999 on Royal Academy label on reverse
Oil on canvas
44 x 57 inches
Provenance: The Estate of Peter Coker
Literature: *Royal Academy Illustrated*, 1999, page 74;
Peter Coker RA, London: Chris Beetles, 2002, pages 109 and 141, Catalogue Raisonné no 558
Exhibited: Royal Academy, Summer Exhibition, 1999, no 356;
'Peter Coker RA', Chris Beetles Gallery, London, October 2002, no 127;
'Peter Coker RA: the Studio Sale', Chris Beetles Gallery, London, October 2017, no 127

SYDNEY HARPLEY

Sydney Harpley, RA FRBS (1927-1992)

The work of Sydney Harpley always surprised and delighted: dancers, acrobats, girls on swings were posed and executed with equal audacity and elegance. Establishing the single female as his favourite subject while still a student, he rose to become the most popular sculptor, not only among Royal Academicians but among all who exhibited at the Royal Academy Summer Exhibitions.

For a biography of Sydney Harpley, please refer to *Chris Beetles Summer Show*, 2015, page 67.

Chris Beetles Gallery represents the Estate of Sydney Harpley.

123
Ondine
Signed and numbered 7/12 (on rock)
Bronze
4 ½ x 7 x 3 ¾ inches
Exhibited: Duncalfe Fine Art, Harrogate, 1988, no 2; 'Sydney Harpley RA. New Sculptures', Chris Beetles Gallery, London, 1990, no 17

Number seven from an edition of twelve.
On a travertine base measuring 4 ½ x 3 ½ x ½ inches

124
Early Sunbather
Signed and numbered 2/12 (on left hip)
Bronze
2 x 4 ¾ x 1 ¼ inches
Provenance: The Artist's Estate
Exhibited: 'Exhibition of Sculpture and Drawings by Sydney Harpley', South African Association of Arts, Capetown, June 1965, no 14 or 15

Number two from an edition of twelve
On a slate base measuring 5 x 1 ½ x ½ inches

125 (right)
The Sunbather
Signed, inscribed 'Provence St Victor des Oules' and dated 1971
Watercolour
15 ¼ x 20 ¾ inches

St-Victor-des-Oules is a village in Provence, near the medieval village of Uzès. During the 1960's-1970's Sydney Harpley owned a holiday home there and was inspired, over several years, to produce a series of bronzes and watercolours of sunbathers, often nude and slumbering under large sun hats.

126 (below)
'The Terrace' St Victor des Oules
Inscribed with title on original backboard
Oil on board
16 x 18 ½ inches
Provenance: Leonie Jonleigh Studio, October 1978;
Mrs John Hudson-Lyons

DONALD HAMILTON FRASER

Donald Hamilton Fraser, RA (1929-2009)

His boldly-handled and richly-coloured semi-abstracts, influenced by the School of Paris, established Donald Hamilton Fraser as one of the most distinctive British Modernist painters of the immediate post-war generation.

For a biography of Donald Hamilton Fraser, please refer to *Chris Beetles Summer Show,* 2012, page 23.

127
In Turbulent Seas
Signed with monogram
Oil on paper
11 ½ x 17 inches

128
Velocity
Signed with initials
Signed with initials on stretcher
Oil on canvas
18 ¼ x 24 ¼ inches

KEITH GRANT

Keith Frederick Grant (born 1930)

One of the greatest living British landscape painters, Keith Grant has travelled extensively, and has confronted the elements in order to produce extraordinary, resonant images of nature, especially in the north. Recently, he has preferred to recollect his experiences in the tranquility of his studio in Norway, and work imaginatively to produce an exciting series of what he calls 'autobiographical' paintings.

For a biography of Keith Grant, please refer to *Chris Beetles Summer Show*, 2015, page 55.

Chris Beetles Gallery represented Keith Grant between 2009-2021. They held the highly successful solo shows, 'Elements of the Earth', in April 2010, 'Metamorphosis', in April 2016, 'North by New English' in June 2017, 'Antarctica' in October 2018 and 'Invention & Variation' in March 2020.

129
Rock and Moon, Judea, Israel
Signed, inscribed with title and dated 88 on reverse
Acrylic on board
14 ¼ x 19 inches

'The artist's visit to Israel was the inspiration of Norman Hyams, one of Grant's most staunch patrons and owner of some of his best paintings. As an admirer of the Norwegian and tropical landscapes in particular, he wondered how Grant would respond to painting the deserts of Israel. The visit lasted for just over four weeks in April/May 1988, when Grant was given leave of absence from his position as head of the art department at Roehampton Institute of Higher Education, and was sponsored by the British Israel Art Foundation, which promotes Israeli culture, and the Ben Gurion University Trust.'

(Ian Simpson, 'Keith Grant in Israel', *The Artist*, June 1989, page 12)

130
Winter Cloud, Norway
Signed
Inscribed with title on reverse
Oil on canvas
43 ¼ x 58 ¾ inches

The Narrow Road to the Deep North

Keith Grant has constantly enriched his experience and understanding of the North by engaging with the responses of other creative figures, and particularly composers and writers. One of the most important of these responses for him has been *The Narrow Road to the Deep North* by Matsuo Bashō (1644-1694), in which the seventeenth-century Japanese poet described a journey using *haibun*, a literary form combining prose and haiku poetry. Though Bashō's journey took place in the Oku region of Japan, Keith was able to use it as both a counterpoint and a control for his own travels in Scotland, Northern Ireland and especially Norway. 'The Narrow Road to the Deep North' became the umbrella title for a group of works on paper, as represented by the present examples, which he discussed in his journal. While 'planning a voyage to the far North in winter' (17 October 1971), and specifically to Norway, he recorded that he was

'working on a series of watercolours and inks, each work being associated with a verse from Bashō's The Narrow Road to the Deep North ... The watercolours are among the best things I have produced: something of the humility of Bashō's reflections upon nature and his sublime ordered expression have influenced them. I expect to be under this influence for some time for it is a key which has enabled me to pass through the first gate to my journey.'

(in his journal, 27 November 1971)

The results appeared in his major exhibition – also called 'The Narrow Road to the Deep North' – which was organised by the Scottish Arts Council, and toured Edinburgh, Strathclyde, Milngavie and Aberdeen, between November 1973 and April 1974. The centrepiece of the exhibition was a series of 24 canvases representing a continuous horizon of the north Norwegian coastline, with each picture standing for one hour of the day.

Keith Grant: *Metamorphosis*, London: Chris Beetles, 2016, pages 30-31.

Nos **131-136** were all exhibited in
'The Narrow Road to the Deep North:
An Exhibition of Paintings by Keith Grant',
Scottish Arts Council, Edinburgh, 1973

132
The Road to Cold Mountain
Signed, inscribed and dated 1972
Acrylic with ink and watercolour
14 x 10 ½ inches
Exhibited: Rochdale Libraries & Arts Services, 1972;
'The Narrow Road to the Deep North', 1973, no 26

131
Dull Spring
The Road to Snaefellsjokull – Iceland
Signed, inscribed with title and dated 1973
Acrylic with ink and watercolour
5 ¾ x 8 ¼ inches
Exhibited: 'The Narrow Road to the Deep North', 1973, no 54

133
Snaefellsjokull and cloud with old lava in foreground, Iceland
Signed, inscribed with title and dated 73
Acrylic with ink and watercolour
6 ½ x 6 ½ inches
Exhibited: 'The Narrow Road to the Deep North', 1973, no 41

134
The Road to Snaefellsjokull – Iceland Rain and Melt Lake
Signed, inscribed with title and dated 9/73
Acrylic with ink and watercolour
7 ¾ x 8 ¾ inches
Exhibited: The Rochdale Libraries and Arts Services, 1973;
'The Narrow Road to the Deep North', 1973, no 31

135
Entrance to Snaefellsjokull – Iceland, June
Signed, inscribed with title and dated 73
Acrylic with ink and watercolour
4 ¾ x 5 ¾ inches
Exhibited: 'The Narrow Road to the Deep North', 1973, no 40

136
Snow-melt patterns like animal forms
Signed, inscribed with title and dated 'June 1973'
Acrylic with ink and watercolour
10 ½ x 13 ¾ inches
Exhibited: 'The Narrow Road to the Deep North', 1973, no 29

ANTHONY GREEN

Anthony Eric Sandall Green, RA Hon RBA
Hon ROI LG NEAC (1939-2023)

No visitor to the Royal Academy Summer Exhibition could have overlooked the work of the painter and printmaker, Anthony Green. His large, irregularly shaped oils rehearse the experience of his life, and especially his marriage, with exuberance, humour and passion.

For a biography of Anthony Green, please refer to
Chris Beetles Summer Show, 2016, pages 60-61.

137
Poppies II: Will You Marry Me Again and Again?
Signed, inscribed with title and dimensions in inches,
and dated 2015 on reverse
Oil on shaped board
28 x 59 ¾ inches
Literature: Martin Bailey (ed), *Anthony Green: Painting Life*,
London: Royal Academy of Arts, 2017, pages 158-159,
Catalogue Raisonné no AG585
Exhibited: Royal Academy Summer Exhibition, London, 2019, no 373

A Life Lived in Love and Paint
Remembering Anthony Green RA

The world is a less sunny and interesting place since Anthony Green died on Valentine's Day in 2023. All his energy and eccentricity and a lifelong love affair with his wife Mary was expressed through arresting pictures of great power and invention.

All this will be recalled and celebrated with a comprehensive retrospective exhibition in October 2025. It will trace this remarkable painter's progress from student life at the Slade to triumphant days at the Royal Academy.

28 October – 15 November 2025

A fully-illustrated catalogue will accompany the exhibition and will contain a new monograph by William Packer NEAC, author, art critic and painter.

138

Pink Vase of Flowers on a Provençal Cloth, a Head Full of Flowers II
Signed, inscribed with title and dated 2013 on reverse
Oil on shaped board
22 ¾ x 25 inches
Literature: Martin Bailey (ed), *Anthony Green: Painting Life*, London:
Royal Academy of Arts, 2017, page 142, Catalogue Raisonné no AG565
Exhibited: Royal Academy, Summer Exhibition, London, 2014, as 'a Head Full of Flowers II';
'Looking Back with Anthony Green', Chris Beetles Gallery, London, January-March 2017

VAL ARCHER

Val Archer (born 1946)

Blurring distinctions between still life, interior and the record of architectural detail, Val Archer has developed a highly original and absorbing body of work. Attentive to the aesthetic pleasures of life, she handles paint sensitively and sensuously, and keeps alive the canvas and paper through thrilling combinations of colour, texture and motif. Flowers, fruits and fabrics are set against complex, resonant surfaces to encapsulate feelings for places and cultures.

For a biography of Val Archer, please refer to Chris Beetles Summer Show, 2024, page 148.

139
Pomegranate Flowers in Green Glazed Jug
Signed with initials
Oil on board
10 x 8 inches

140 (below left)
Peonies in Chinese Vase
Signed with initials
Oil on paper
18 ¼ x 15 inches

141 (below)
Pink Camellias and Fresco of Saints
Signed with initials
Oil on board
15 x 11 inches

142
**Camellias and Flemish Still-life Painters
of the 17th Century**
Signed with initials
Oil on paper
16 ½ x 17 ¼ inches

VAL ARCHER

143
Almonds in Pugliese Jug
Signed with initials
Oil on paper
30 ¼ x 20 ¼ inches

LESLEY FOTHERBY

Lesley Fotherby (born 1946)

Multi-talented and multi-faceted, Lesley Fotherby goes from strength to strength in expanding her range and increasing her popularity. She perpetually strives to capture the moving world around her, with fresh approaches and new appeal.

For a biography of Lesley Fotherby, please refer to *Chris Beetles Summer Show*, 2024, page 149.

144
Magnolias, Kew
Signed
Inscribed with title on reverse
Oil on canvas
18 x 24 inches

LESLEY FOTHERBY

145 (left)
**Vineyard at San Quirico,
Looking Towards San Gimignano**
Signed
Inscribed with title on stretcher
Oil on canvas
24 x 30 inches

146 (below)
The Blue Mountains, Aptera, Crete
Signed
Inscribed with title on reverse
Oil on canvas
14 x 18 inches

GERALDINE GIRVAN

Geraldine Girvan (born 1947)

Geraldine Girvan has been exhibiting at Chris Beetles Gallery for over thirty five years and, in that time, she has consistently proven that the strong tradition of Scottish colourists is still very much alive.

For a biography of Geraldine Girvan, please refer to *Chris Beetles Summer Show,* 2024, page 150.

147
Late Afternoon
Signed and dated 1991
Signed, inscribed with title and dated 'Jan 1991' on reverse
Watercolour
29 ½ x 39 inches
Provenance: Barry Bernstein Collection
Exhibited: 'Geraldine Girvan', Chris Beetles Gallery, London, March 1993, no 25

148 (left)
Dried Flowers on a Blue Cloth
Signed and dated 24
Signed, inscribed with title and dimensions and dated 'Feb 2024' on reverse
Watercolour and bodycolour
15 x 30 inches

149 (below)
Late Summer Still Life
Signed
Signed and inscribed with title and dimensions on reverse
Oil on linen
24 x 24 inches

150
Houseman at the Window
Signed
Signed, inscribed with title and dimensions
and dated 2024 on reverse
Oil on linen
28 x 34 inches

MELISSA SCOTT-MILLER

Melissa Scott-Miller, RBA RP NEAC (born 1959)

Melissa Scott-Miller is an acclaimed painter of meticulously detailed urban landscapes and portraits of people in their surroundings.

For a biography of Melissa Scott-Miller, please refer to *Chris Beetles Summer Show*, 2024, page 150.

151
Magnolia outside St James's Church
Signed with initials and dated 25
Oil on canvas
19 ¾ x 27 ½ inches

'Had such a lovely time painting around St James's and Mayfair, mainly in the sunshine! The one I painted of the magnolia outside St James's church was tricky as I often had to wait for vans to come and go, but so lovely that bus drivers would stop leaving a gap so I could still see, and shout words of encouragement! Also wonderful that I could keep my wet canvases at Chris Beetles Gallery and get cups of tea in between painting ...'

152
Spring Blossom, Cadogan Gardens
Signed with initials and dated 25
Oil on canvas
11 ¾ x 31 ¼ inches

'Finished this today, painted over four days. I was very lucky with the blossom coming out at exactly the right time and the weather! And a very lovely lady who offered me tea from the taxi driver hut. A view that I've seen from the bus many times ...
Hope to do lots of interesting views of London, so many that I've always wanted to paint!'

153
Cherry Blossom Spring, St James's Square
Signed with initials and dated 25
Oil on canvas
16 x 20 inches

154 (left)
Early Spring, Cheyne Walk
Signed with initials and dated 25
Oil on canvas
19 ¾ x 23 ¾ inches

'I've been enjoying trying to capture the spring sunlight on these beautiful historic houses in Cheyne Walk. I find them very romantic and I think about the incredible people who have lived there like Rossetti and Whistler, it was lovely and peaceful there, I felt transported to another world!'

155 (below)
Wisteria, Cheyne Walk
Signed with initials and dated 25
Oil on canvas
20 x 24 inches

146

156
Beginning of Spring, Islington
Signed with initials and dated 25
Oil on canvas
24 x 30 inches

MELISSA SCOTT-MILLER

157 (left)
The Warrington, Maida Vale
Signed with initials and dated 25
Oil on canvas
11 ¾ x 15 ¾ inches

158 (below)
Early Spring, The Warrington, Maida Vale
Signed with initials and dated 25
Oil on canvas
16 x 20 inches

JACK RUSSELL

Jack Russell, MBE (born 1963)

After a highly successful career as an international Test cricketer, rising to become England's greatest wicketkeeper, Jack Russell has grown into an acclaimed painter of atmospheric landscapes, idyllic cricketing scenes and stirring portraits. In recent years, he has focused on a series of powerful portraits of war heroes and veterans.

159
The Warrington Fox, Maida Vale
Signed
Signed, inscribed 'The Warrington Fox' and dated 2025 on reverse
Oil on canvas
16 x 24 inches

Johnny Johnson the Last Dambuster

'Johnny Johnson was the last surviving member of the RAF who took part in the famous Dambuster's Raid by 617 Squadron in 1943. He was a bomb aimer, and was detailed to deliver one of inventor Barnes Wallis's bouncing bombs. On the day of the raid, the Rur dam his plane was required to bomb was changed last minute, the significance being they had practised their bombing raids front on, but the Sorpe Dam had to be attacked from the side, dropping the bomb on top of the middle of the dam wall. His plane had to fly near to a hillside then dive steeply down very close to a church steeple and drop the bomb as low as possible dead centre. Being such a perfectionist, bomb aimer Johnny made the Captain of the Lancaster continuously take the highly dangerous flying manoeuvre ten times before he was happy to release the bomb. Much to his fellow crew members relief! Of the 19 Lancaster bombers that took part in the raid, only 11 returned. 53 of Johnny's fellow 617 Squadron members were killed and 3 were taken prisoner. He went on to take part in 19 other bombing raids with 617 Squadron. After the war he remained with the RAF, retiring in 1962 with the rank of Squadron Leader. He became a primary school teacher and a teacher at a psychiatric hospital. He later moved to Torquay where he took an interest in politics and became a local councillor. He passed away in December 2022 at the age of 101.

I had wanted to paint Johnny for quite some time and had spent several years looking around the country for him to find that he only lived a few miles down the road from me in Bristol! I finally found him in August 2022 just a few months before he passed away. To paint the portrait of the last surviving member of the famous Dambusters Raid was an absolute privilege but the most mesmerising part of the experience was to sit and chat with him and listen to the most amazing life story. Priceless.'

Jack Russell, MBE

Detail of [160]

160
Johnny Johnson the Last Dambuster
Signed and inscribed with title
Signed, inscribed with title, '7.8. by Johnny Johnson', 'Johnny Johnson MBE, DFC signed for me at his care home Westbury-on-Trym, Bristol, Jack Russell, 2022', and dated 2022 on reverse
Oil on canvas
30 x 35 inches
Exhibited: Royal Society of Portrait Painters, Annual Exhibition, Mall Galleries, London, May 2025

"Johnny Johnson, The Last Dambuster"

Joe Collett

'A *Times* newspaper journalist recently said to me during an interview with me about my veteran portraits, "You know you're giving these war veterans therapy don't you?". I hadn't realised before and it was never my intention to do so, that was not the motivation behind the project, but since he mentioned it I've come to realise that he may be right.
My portrait of Joe Collett is a prime example. He was part of my self-imposed challenge to paint the last surviving members of the Gloucestershire Regiment who fought at the famous Battle of the Imjin River, Korean War, 1951.
(My driving instructor was there, that's how I became interested in that particular battle). The regiment were surrounded for several days by tens of thousands of Chinese soldiers until eventually most of the regiment were either killed or taken prisoner. A few escaped back to friendly lines but not many. Two Victoria Crosses were awarded for the action. Joe Collett was there. He was wounded in the hand and legs early in the battle and was evacuated back to friendly lines in an ambulance. All the other veterans who I painted from the battle were eventually taken prisoner. This has always troubled Joe. He has always felt extremely guilty that he survived and got out before it was too late. Many of his friends were killed or captured. When I wanted to paint him, I was told that it may not be possible, he may not agree. I learned that he wasn't really one for regimental reunions and didn't like doing interviews. He pretty much kept himself to himself. But he is a sports fan, in particular cricket and football. So when he heard that it was an ex-Gloucestershire and England cricketer who wanted to paint him, he agreed to do it. The veteran portraits are normally for me two sittings. The first sitting is short. Just a chat and a few photographs (for reference). The second is much longer, around three hours, where I paint a small colour sketch to take back to the studio as reference for the larger, final portrait. Joe was very accommodating but you could tell he was very wary of the whole situation and wasn't overly conversational when it came to chatting about what happened at the battle. I could see it was difficult for him to go back there in his mind.
I took the necessary photographs and left him in peace. During the second sitting, while I was painting the colour sketch, he slowly opened up and began explaining, gradually, in more detail, what actually happened. I was so engrossed in what he was saying that I hardly painted at all for a while and just let him release all that hidden information. Information he had kept to himself for 70 years. I could see how difficult this was for him. It became even more difficult when he began to talk about his son who had also served with the army, this time in the Grenadier Guards. The reason it was so difficult was because his son was no longer alive. I could see the pain and torment in Joe's face as I painted him. The anguish in his eyes. After a couple of hours I stopped painting and left the colour sketch unfinished. But to me it is finished. Because once I had captured that look of pain in Joes eyes I knew I had captured the very essence of what I was after. When Joe stood up again at the end of the sitting he seemed to stand taller than before. He even began to show a smile for the first time. He looked much more relaxed. More at peace. In fact his demeanour has changed considerably. We even joked and laughed about the world in general. It was an amazing transformation. So much so that in the final portrait, although there is still a little anguish in Joe's eyes, there is a hint of a smile. A man in a better place. To totally appreciate the look in Joe's eyes in the colour sketch you need to have heard the whole story from him first hand. To hear the outpouring of pain to really understand that look in his eye. But the emotion is there. The pain of guilt and grief. Guilt that he got out of the battle early and was forced to leave his mates to die or suffer the 2 years depravation of a Chinese prisoner of war camp. And grief for the loss of a son at such an early age. I've met Joe several times since at various regimental reunions and get togethers. The scars are still there but he is now someone more at peace and with less weight on his shoulders. There's even a joke and a smile from him from time to time. The driving force behind painting war veterans for me is simple. To make sure that what they went through, their sacrifice, is never forgotten. It's as simple as that for me. Capturing their character on canvas is the best way I know of making sure that happens. After we are all gone, the portraits will still be here. Caught on canvas forever.'
Jack Russell MBE

161
Joe Collett, Colour Sketch
Signed
Signed twice, inscribed with title, 'War Veteran, Gloucestershire Regiments. Present at the Battle of the Injin River 1951', 'painted from life Cheltenham' and 'painted for the book "Final Roll Call" published by Soldiers of Gloucestershire Museum 2023',
and dated 2022 on reverse
Oil on canvas
12 x 10 inches

CUMULATIVE INDEX OF ARTISTS

CHRIS BEETLES SUMMER SHOWS 1998-2025

A
Abbott, John White: 2001
Ackermann, Gerald: 1999, 2006, 2025
Akhriev, Daud: 2012
Allan, Robert Weir: 2019
Alexander, William: 2020
Allingham, Helen: 1998, 1999, 2002, 2004, 2005, 2016, 2017, 2018, 2020, 2021, 2024
Anderson, Robert: 2019
Anderson, Stanley: 2017, 2018, 2024, 2025
Angus, John: 2017
Annigoni, Pietro: 2003, 2016, 2018
Archer, Frank: 1998
Archer, Val: 2024, 2025
Ardizzone, Edward: 1998, 2000
Armfield, Maxwell: 2003
Atcherley, Ethel: 2000, 2024, 2025
Aumonier, James: 2021
Austin, Robert Sargent: 2006, 2008, 2017
Ayrton, Michael: 2000, 2001

B
Badmin, Stanley Roy: 1998, 1999, 2000, 2001, 2002, 2003, 2004, 2005, 2006, 2008, 2010, 2012, 2015, 2016, 2017, 2018, 2019, 2024, 2025
Balmer, George: 2017
Barry, Claude Francis: 2002
Bartlett, William Henry: 2002, 2016
Barton, Mary: 2000
Barton, Rose: 1998, 1999, 2000, 2001, 2004, 2008, 2014, 2015, 2017, 2018, 2019, 2020
Batchelor, Roland: 1998, 2000, 2002, 2003, 2004, 2010
Bawden, Edward: 2006, 2015
Benett, Newton: 1998, 2003
Beresford, Daisy Radcliffe: 2024
Beresford, Louisa Anne: 2001, 2003, 2004, 2021
Bevan, Robert: 2002
Birch, Lamorna: 1999
Blampied, Edmund: 2014, 2017
Bland, Emily Beatrice: 2001, 2019
Bond, William Joseph Julius Caesar: 2017, 2018
Bone, David Muirhead: 1998
Bone, Stephen: 2003
Booth, Raymond: 2018, 2019, 2024
Bourne, James: 2001
Brabazon, Hercules Brabazon: 1998, 1999, 2000, 2001, 2002, 2003, 2005, 2006, 2008, 2010, 2013, 2015, 2016, 2018, 2019, 2020, 2021, 2024, 2025
Brangwyn, Frank: 2001, 2024
Branwhite, Charles: 2004, 2017
Branwhite, Charles Brooke: 2006
Breakspeare, William: 2018
Brett, John: 1998
Brewtnall, Edward Frederick: 2010
Bridge, Elizabeth: 2018
Bright, Henry: 1998
Brill, Reginald: 2002, 2012, 2017
Brittan, Charles Edward: 2002
Buckley, John Edmund: 2025
Burleigh, Averil: 1998
Burne-Jones, Edward: 1999
Butler, James: 2015, 2016, 2017, 2019, 2024
Butler, Mildred Anne: 2014

C
Caffieri, Hector: 2006, 2021, 2025
Callow, William: 1999, 2002
Calthrop, Claude: 2018
Cameron, Katharine: 2025
Camp, Jeffrey: 2001
Canziani, Estella: 1999
Carelli, Gabriele: 1998, 2014, 2019, 2020
Carmichael, John Wilson: 2021
Carter, Henry Barlow: 2002
Casson, Michael: 1998
Chadwick, Ernest Albert: 2001, 2021
Chalon, John James: 2018
Chambers, Alice Mary: 1998, 2020
Churchyard, Thomas: 1998
Clark, Norman: 1999
Clarke, William Hanna: 1998
Clausen, George: 1998, 2003
Clennell, Luke: 2001
Cliff, Clarice: 1998
Clough, Tom: 2024
Coker, Peter: 1998, 1999, 2000, 2003, 2004, 2006, 2008, 2010, 2015, 2025
Cole, George: 2021
Cole, Vicat: 1998, 2000
Coleridge, F G: 1998
Compton, Edward Harrison: 1998, 2002
Compton, Edward Theodore: 1998, 2000, 2021
Connard, Philip: 1998
Constable, John: 2024

Cotman, Miles Edmund: 2019
Cotman, John Sell: 2019
Cox, David: 2001, 2002, 2010, 2017, 2020
Crane, Walter: 2002
Crawford, Ebenezer: 2017
Creswick, Thomas: 2017
Critchlow, Michael Bernard: 2025
Cromek, Thomas Hartley: 1998
Crouch, William: 1998, 2017, 2018, 2019
Cundall, Charles: 2002, 2025

D

Da Costa, John: 2000
Day, Paul: 2006, 2008
Dayes, Edward: 1998, 2001, 2020
Delaborde, Henri: 2018
De Wint, Peter: 2002
Dey de Ribcowsky, Richard: 2019
Dick, Sir William Reid: 2006
Dixon, Charles: 1998
Dobson, William Charles Thomas: 2019, 2025
Dodgson, George Haydock: 2017, 2018
Doré, Gustave: 1998
Downman, John: 2001, 2020, 2021
Drewry, Judith Holmes: 2001
Dunlop, Jessie: 2008, 2025
Dunstan, Bernard: 2002, 2003, 2019, 2024, 2025

E

Earle, Charles: 1999
East, Alfred: 1998
Eaton, Maria: 2020
Elgood, George Samuel: 1998, 2021
Elwyn, John: 2003
Evans, Bernard Walter: 2018
Eyton, Anthony: 2018

F

Farrell, Fred: 2004
Field, Walter: 2018
Fielding, Copley: 2020
Fielding, Newton: 2018
Fisk, William Henry: 2019
Flint, Francis Russell: 2018
Flint, William Russell: 1998, 1999
Foster, Myles Birket: 1998, 1999, 2001, 2002, 2004, 2017, 2019, 2020, 2021, 2024
Fotherby, Lesley: 2006, 2024, 2025
Franz, Ettore Roesler: 2021
Fraser, Arthur Anderson: 2010
Fraser, Donald Hamilton: 2006, 2012, 2015, 2025

Fraser, Francis Arthur: 2025
Fraser, Gilbert Baird: 2006, 2010, 2020
Fraser, Gordon: 2015, 2018
Fraser, Robert Winchester: 2006, 2010, 2015
Frost, William Edward: 2015, 2017
Fulleylove, John: 2000, 2005, 2019, 2021

G

Garden, William Fraser: 2006, 2010, 2015, 2018
Gill, Eric: 2008
Gillray, James: 2021
Ginger, Phyllis: 2006
Girtin, Thomas: 2024
Girvan, Geraldine: 2006, 2024, 2025
Glindoni, Henry Gillard: 2018
Glover, John: 1998, 2019
Goodall, Edward Angelo: 2021
Goodwin, Albert: 1998, 1999, 2000, 2001, 2002, 2003, 2005, 2006, 2008, 2010, 2011, 2012, 2013, 2014, 2015, 2016, 2017, 2018, 2019, 2020, 2021, 2024, 2025
Goodwin, Harry: 1999, 2002, 2019
Gordon-Cumming, Constance Frederica: 2014, 2015, 2016, 2020, 2021, 2024
Gore, Frederick: 2001
Gore, William Henry: 2002
Gosling, William: 2005
Gosse, Sylvia: 2003
Gow, Mary: 2001
Grant, Carleton: 2002, 2018
Grant, Keith: 2008, 2010, 2011, 2012, 2013, 2014, 2015, 2018, 2025
Gray, James: 2002
Green, Charles: 2020, 2021
Green, Anthony: 2015, 2016, 2017, 2019, 2025
Greenham, Peter: 2001
Gregory, Edward John: 2005
Griggs, Frederick Landseer Maur: 2024
Grimshaw, John Atkinson: 2002, 2013
Grolleron, Paul: 2018

H

Hagedorn, Karl: 1998, 2012, 2017, 2018
Haghe, Louis: 2002
Hale, William Matthew: 1998
Halfpenny, Joseph: 2002
Handley-Read, Edward: 2024
Hardy, Frederick Daniel: 2003
Hardy, Thomas Bush: 2004, 2005
Hardwick, John Jessop: 2005, 2010
Hare, Augustus: 1998
Hare, St George: 2000

Harper, Edward Steel: 2008, 2010, 2014, 2017, 2025
Harpley, Sydney: 1998, 2003, 2004, 2006, 2010, 2012, 2015, 2016, 2019, 2024, 2025
Harris, Edwin: 2000, 2017
Harris, Totosha: 2025
Hastie, Grace: 1998
Hatherell, William: 2025
Hay, James Hamilton: 2017, 2018, 2019
Hayter, John: 2001
Hearne, Thomas: 2018
Hennell, Thomas: 1998, 2006, 2012
Hennessy, Patrick: 2018
Henshall, John Henry: 2004
Henshaw, Frederick: 2017, 2025
Hewitt, Beatrice: 2020
Hilder, Rowland: 1998, 2012, 2024
Hill, James John: 2019, 2024
Hills, Robert: 1998, 2002
Holloway, Charles Edward: 2000
Hopkins, Arthur: 2015
Hopper, Charles: 1998
Hornsey, John: 2017
Horsley, Thomas: 2001
Hough, William: 2002, 2018
Houston, John Adam: 2002, 2025
Howard, George: 2018, 2019
Howard, Norman: 2025
Huggins, William: 1998, 2017
Hughes, Arthur: 2000, 2005
Hughes, Edward Robert: 1998
Hunn, Thomas: 2004
Hunt, Alfred William: 1998, 2000, 2004, 2005, 2006, 2013, 2018, 2019, 2024
Hunt, Cecil Arthur: 1998, 1999, 2000, 2002, 2004, 2006, 2008, 2010, 2015, 2016, 2018, 2024
Hunt, William Henry: 1998, 1999, 2002, 2003, 2005, 2006, 2010, 2018
Hunt, William Holman: 2004

I

Ibbetson, Julius Caesar: 2017

J

Jackson, John: 2019
James, Francis: 1998
John, Gwen: 1999
Johnson, Edward Killingworth: 2018, 2024
Jonzen, Karin: 2003, 2006
Joseph, Lily Delissa: 2000
Joyce, Richard: 1998
Jutsum, Henry: 2018

K

Kapp, Edmond: 2008
Kelly, Gerald: 2000
Kilburne, George Goodwin: 1998, 2010, 2017, 2018, 2025
Kirkpatrick, Joseph: 1998
Klinghoffer, Clara: 2003
Knight, Charles: 1998, 2004, 2008, 2015, 2017, 2018, 2024
Knight, Geraldine: 2002
Knight, Harold: 2020
Knight, Laura: 2000
Koch, Gabriele: 1998

L

Lamplough, Augustus: 1998
Landseer, Charles: 2002
La Thangue, Henry Herbert: 2010, 2025
Lear, Edward: 1998, 2010, 2013, 2014, 2016, 2017, 2018, 2019, 2020, 2021
Leaver, Noel Harry: 1998
Le Blanc, Lloyd: 2001, 2006, 2019
Lee, Frederick Walter: 1998
Leitch, Richard Principal: 1998
Lessieux, Ernest: 2018
Lines, Vincent: 2012
Linnell, James: 2001
Lloyd, Tom: 1998
Lucas, Arthur: 2005
Lushington, Franklin: 2020, 2021

M

Macbeth, Robert Walker: 2005, 2020
Macdonald, William Alister: 2001, 2006, 2017
MacWhirter, John: 2014
Mann, Alexander: 2017
Margetson, William Henry: 2021
Marks, George: 2006, 2020
Markes, Albert: 1998
Markino, Yoshio: 2004
Marshall, Herbert Menzies: 1998, 2000, 2004, 2010, 2014, 2018, 2020, 2025
Martineau, Edith: 2016, 2017, 2024, 2025
McCoy, Ann Wyeth: 2019
McFall, David: 2002
Menpes, Mortimer: 1998
Miller, William Rickarby: 2019
Minton, John: 1999
Montalba, Clara: 1999
Moorcroft, William: 1998
Moore, Henry: 2000, 2003, 2017, 2018
Morgan, Walter Jenks: 1999

Mote, George William: 2018
Muller, William James: 2017
Muncaster, Claude: 2006
Munn, Paul Sandby: 2001
Murray, David: 2002
Muschamp, Francis Sydney: 2010
Mycock, William: 1998

N
Naish, John George: 2018
Nash, John: 1998, 2002, 2003
Nash, Paul: 1998
Neasom, Norman: 1998, 1999, 2010, 2016, 2025
Nicholls, George Frederick: 2014
Nicholson, Francis: 2017, 2018, 2019
Nisbet, Robert Buchan: 2018
Nixon, Job: 2024
Nixon, John: 2021, 2025
Norris, Hugh: 2010
North, John William: 2000, 2005, 2014

O
O'Neil, Henry Nelson: 2006, 2024
O'Neill, George Bernard: 2003
Orrock, James: 1998, 1999, 2017
Osborn, Emily Mary: 2018
Owen, Samuel: 2019

P
Palmer, Sutton: 1998
Pars, William: 2002
Parsons, Alfred: 2000, 2016, 2019, 2020, 2021, 2025
Parsons, Beatrice: 1998, 2000, 2003, 2004, 2005, 2010, 2025
Paterson, Caroline: 2018
Paton, Joseph Noel: 1999, 2020
Paton, Waller Hugh: 2017, 2018
Payne, William: 2001, 2024
Peake, Mervyn: 1998, 1999, 2025
Pellegrini, Carlo: 2024
Pemberton, Muriel: 1998, 2013
Petit, John Louis: 2013
Philpot, Glyn: 2006
Pickersgill, Frederick Richard: 2017, 2019
Pinwell, George John: 2025
Piper, John: 1998, 1999, 2002, 2003, 2006, 2010, 2015, 2018
Pisa, Alberto: 2024
Plazzotta, Enzo: 2002, 2003, 2004, 2010, 2012, 2024
Prout, John Skinner: 2002, 2021
Prout, Samuel: 1999, 2024
Prout, Samuel Gillespie: 2024
Pyne, George: 2001, 2017, 2020

Pyne, James Baker: 2021

R
Rackham, Arthur: 1998, 2002
Rainey, William: 2017
Rainford, Edward: 2003
Rayner, Louise: 1998, 1999, 2004, 2025
Rayner, Margaret: 2025
Rayner, Samuel: 2025
Read, Samuel: 2020
Reynolds, Alan: 2001, 2002, 2003
Richards, Ceri: 1998, 1999, 2000, 2003, 2006
Richards, John Inigo: 2019
Richardson, Charles James: 2001
Richardson, Thomas Miles: 2001
Richmond, William Blake: 1998
Roberts, David: 2013
Roberts, Henry Benjamin: 1998
Roberts-Jones, Ivor: 2003
Robertson, Charles: 2019
Romeril, Nicholas: 2012
Rosoman, Leonard: 2000, 2003
Rothenstein, Michael: 2001
Rothenstein, William: 2003
Roussoff, Alexandre Nicolaievitch: 2003
Rowbotham, Thomas Leeson: 2004
Rowe, Ernest Arthur: 2019
Rowlandson, Thomas: 1998, 2001, 2002, 2010, 2017, 2018, 2019, 2020, 2021, 2024, 2025
Royal Doulton: 1998
Rushbury, Henry: 1998
Ruskin, John: 2025
Russell, Jack: 2025
Russell, John: 2025

S
Salisbury, Frank O: 2015
Sargent, John Singer: 1998
Schwabe, Randolph: 1998, 2000, 2017, 2024
Scott-Miller, Melissa: 2024, 2025
Seago, Edward: 1998, 2002, 2003, 2004, 2005
Seel, Adolf: 2018
Severn, Arthur: 2000
Sheffield, George: 2006
Shepard, Ernest Howard: 2001, 2002, 2017
Shepherd, David: 2020
Shepherd, George Sidney: 1998
Shepherd, Thomas Hosmer: 2014, 2018
Sheringham, George: 2025
Sherrin, John: 1998, 1999, 2000, 2002, 2003, 2004, 2006, 2018, 2024
Simeon, Harry: 1998

Simmons, John: 2005, 2019
Simpson, Charles Walter: 2002 [RBA RI ROI]
Simpson, Charles Walter: 2002 [RCANA]
Simpson, William: 1998, 2000, 2004, 2005, 2015, 2018, 2019, 2021, 2025
Skeaping, John: 2003
Smith, Arthur Reginald: 1998, 2003, 2006, 2010, 2012, 2017, 2025
Smith, Carlton Alfred: 1999, 2020, 2025
Smith, Edwin: 2008
Smythe, Lionel Percy: 1998, 2000, 2002, 2004, 2025
Smythe, Minnie: 1998
Snaffles (Charles Johnson Payne): 2025
Solomon, Simeon: 1998
Sorrell, Elizabeth: 1998
Sowerby, John: 1999, 2000, 2018
Speed, Harold: 2025
Spiers, Benjamin Walter: 1999, 2002, 2004, 2005, 2014
Stanfield, Clarkson: 2002, 2018
Stannard, Lilian: 1998
Stannard, Sylvester: 2002
Steer, Philip Wilson: 1998, 2000, 2002, 2004, 2020
Stewart, Janet Cumbrae: 1999, 2003, 2004, 2006, 2012
Stillman, Lisa: 2000
Stroudley, James: 2002, 2006, 2008, 2010
Sutherland, Graham: 2001
Swanwick, Betty: 2006, 2019, 2024
Swete, John: 2002

T

Talmage, Algernon: 2004, 2018
Tayler, Albert Chevallier: 2020
Taylor, Leonard Campbell: 2019
Thompson, David: 2006
Thomson, Alfred Reginald: 2025
Tindle, David: 1998, 2001, 2008
Topham, Frank William Warwick: 2020
Topolski, Feliks: 2006, 2010
Towne, Francis: 2001, 2018
Tuke, Henry Scott: 1998
Tunnicliffe, Charles: 2003, 2017, 2019, 2024
Turner, Joseph Mallord William: 2017, 2024
Turner (of Oxford), William: 1998
Tyndale, Walter: 1998, 1999, 2001, 2003, 2004, 2006, 2021, 2024, 2025

V

Varley, John: 2002, 2015, 2017, 2018, 2019, 2021
Verey, Arthur: 2024
Von Herkomer, Hubert: 2020

W

Wain, Louis: 1998
Waite, Robert Thorne: 2020, 2025
Walcot, William: 1998, 1999, 2002, 2003, 2004, 2006, 2013, 2014, 2016, 2017, 2018, 2020, 2021, 2024
Wallis, Henry: 2003
Ward, John: 1998, 2019
Ward, Leslie: 2021
Ward, Vernon: 2002
Wardle, Arthur: 2010
Warren, Edmund George: 1998, 1999, 2000, 2001, 2003, 2005, 2021, 2024
Waterhouse, Alfred: 2000, 2021
Waterhouse, John William: 2001
Watson, John Dawson: 2017, 2020
Watts, George Frederic: 2020
Watts, James Thomas: 2002, 2024
Weatherill, George: 1998, 2004, 2005, 2006, 2013, 2016, 2017
Webb, William Edward: 2004
Westall, Richard: 2024
Wheatley, Francis: 2024
Wheeler, Charles: 2008
Whitley, Kate: 1998
Whorf, John: 2019
Wiggins, Guy: 2013
Williams, Grecian: 2019
Wilson, Charles Edward: 2025
Wimperis, Edmund Morison: 2019
Wolfe, George: 2018
Wood, John Norris: 2017
Wood, William: 1998
Woodhouse, William: 2017
Woodlock, David: 2002, 2019
Woolmer, Alfred Joseph: 2020
Worth, Leslie: 1999
Wright, Richard Henry: 1998
Wlyd, William: 2017
Wyllie, William Lionel: 1998, 2001, 2004, 2006, 2014, 2015
Wyllie, William Morison: 1999
Wynne, David: 2004

19th Century English School: 2024, 2025
Early 20th Century English School: 2025

INDEX OF ARTISTS

Ackermann, Gerald	79
Anderson, Stanley	94-97
Archer, Val	136-138
Atcherley, Ethel	75
Badmin, Stanley Roy	109-113
Brabazon, Hercules Brabazon	18-22
Buckley, John Edmund	16-17
Caffieri, Hector	66-67
Cameron, Katharine	82-83
Coker, Peter	122-125
Critchlow, Michael Bernard	108
Cundall, Charles	100-101
Dobson, William Charles Thomas	14
Dunlop, Jessie I	107
Dunstan, Bernard	119-121
Fotherby, Lesley	139-140
Fraser, Donald Hamilton	128-129
Fraser, Francis Arthur	58-59
Girvan, Geraldine	141-143
Goodwin, Albert	38-57
Grant, Keith	130-133
Green, Anthony	134-135
Harper, Edward Steel	84-85
Harpley, Sydney	126-127
Harris, Totosha	65
Hatherell, William	72
Henshaw, Frederick Henry	12
Houston, John Adam	13
Howard, Norman	104
Kilburne, George Goodwin	28
La Thangue, Henry Herbert	74
Marshall, Herbert Menzies	29-31
Martineau, Edith	32-33
Neasom, Norman	116-118
Nixon, John	8-9
Parsons, Alfred	60-64
Parsons, Beatrice	78
Peake, Mervyn	114-115
Pinwell, George John	34-36
Rayner, Louise	24
Rayner, Margaret	25
Rayner, Samuel	10-11
Rowlandson, Thomas	6-7
Ruskin, John	15
Russell, Jack	149-153
Russell, John	4-5
Scott-Miller, Melissa	144-148
Sheringham, George	86-93
Simpson, William	23
Smith, Arthur Reginald	76-77
Smith, Carlton Alfred	68-69
Smythe, Lionel Percy	26-27
Snaffles (Charlie Johnson Payne)	98-99
Speed, Harold	80-81
Thomson, Alfred Reginald	102-103
Tyndale, Walter	73
Waite, Robert Thorne	37
Wilson, Charles Edward	70-71
19th Century School	105
20th Century School, Early	106